D1527167

Work: "Only in creative activity do we externalize the identity we have as men made in the image of God. This then is the true basis for work."

Property: "Property rights... exist.... But what is really protected is man's creative mental activity—his ideas which are externalized into things which he owns and has a right to possess and enjoy."

Community: "One person's creative activity is to be qualified by other people's creative activity. Creativity is to be mutually stimulating."

prō·ĕxĭst·ĕnce

Udo Middelmann

the place of man
in the
circle of reality

WIPF & STOCK · Eugene, Oregon

Wipf and Stock Publishers
199 W 8th Ave, Suite 3
Eugene, OR 97401

Pro Existence
The Place of man in the Circle of Reality
By Middelmann, Udo W.
Copyright©1974 by Middelmann, Udo W.
ISBN 13: 978-1-62032-354-0
Publication date 7/15/2012
Previously published by IVP, 1974

To Debby who without ceasing chooses to
create with me our life together

Contents

Preface

Western man's reality has been largely defined by two terms—*materialism* and *technology*. Our wants are material, our method of satisfying them technological. If civil engineering has given us roads and aeronautical engineering has given us the SST, so social and psychological engineering will soon put us at peace with others and at peace with ourselves. Thus thinks technological man.

But many have found this model for man inadequate. And some have opted for its polar opposite: If materialism and technology have failed, let's escape from both. Let's get back to the garden, back to simplicity, back to the small, silent world where the inner self is king.

Many, then, find themselves searching for a purely subjective satisfaction, one totally divorced from any reference to the external world, totally unconcerned with the objectivity of truth. Or, to put it in personal terms, truth is anything that satisfies. Truth is whatever seems true for me.

But the question of objective truth will not go away so easily. Not unless we deny the intellectual aspect of our lives, not unless we refuse to think about what continues to trouble us, sometimes even after we are on our way back to the garden.

What is the case concerning man? Who is he? Who is he really and truly? Can a man be satisfied by an identity not grounded in reality? Can a man long deny the validity of questions about *what is really so?*

The issue is as important for those who call themselves Christians as it is for men in general. For it is possible for Christians to deny their common humanity, to deny their essential relationship to a reality which is there and to escape into a sheer subjective experience or into a small community where an individual's own feelings are affirmed *only* by the small group in which he finds himself.

What is the full circumference of man? What, in fact, is the full circumference of reality? And what is the place of God in that circumference? Does work have value? Does property have value? Where do property rights end and human rights begin? What rights does the community at large have?

If Christianity is true, it must be true in relation to the full circumference of reality, and it must be verifiable in enough areas to be reasonable and therefore credible. The full life of man in the world is the context in which Christianity must be capable of functioning. And this is exactly what we find. Christianity comes down firmly on the side of existence, on the side of the reality of the material as well as the spiritual world.

God is for existence, not against it. And so the title, *Pro-existence*, is meant to suggest the stance of the Christian in the world. But that stance is predicated on a conception of who God is and what his world is like. And that is where we begin.

The Publisher

Creativity
and the
Value
of Work

"Only in creative activity
do we externalize the
identity we have as men
made in the image of
God. This then is the true
basis for work."

1

In the streets of Europe are thousands and thousands of young Europeans and Americans who spend all year doing nothing but hitchhiking from the colder places in the summer to the warmer places in the winter, living out of each other's bags and offering you the shirts off their backs (often they turn out to be your own shirt). They move around in search of an identity, in search of something they can link with their own subjective experience which in itself is not big enough to give them meaning. Often the only identity they find is a series of unrelated experiences, and having these unrelated experiences becomes their absolute, their universal. For them reality has slipped away; man has become the roving creature.

The movie *The Graduate* focuses on Benjamin, a recent college graduate who still does not know who he is. His father asks him repeatedly, "What are you going to do?" Benjamin's concern about this self-identity is pushed aside as his father encourages him to choose an occupation: "What have you graduated for? Why don't you work?" The very real question of Benjamin's identity is done away with, clouded over by the concept of the occupational machine his parents' generation has set forth.

The individuality that Benjamin feels and his need to find a basis for that individuality are replaced by society and its romantically humming, running wheels. We work, we live, we have a swimming pool and four cars, we have enough wives to take turns. Aren't all things going well? Benjamin's "Who am I? What is my purpose?" is replaced by a pattern of society.

Yet some people see the inhumanity of this situation and in brutal honesty move out of it, realizing that the answer to the question of individual identity is not to be found in working five days a week from nine to five. Many have come to L'Abri out of such a background and such a search. And often after they have found their individual identity, what they look for then is a way to express their identity. As Christians, we should understand that their search is right. Any generation has the right to uncover the hypocrisy of a society which pushes only for an occupational choice, a society which would put people into an occupational mold. For oftentimes the occupational choice is set up in order to cloud over the question, "Who am I?"

The fact is that if there is no individual identity, then any job is totally unimportant. Any job becomes a threat to me if it stifles all search and swallows up my individuality, making me indistinguishable from any other cog in society's machine. In such a situation, the job refashions the man, and all that is left for him is never to act but only to react. What is the proper response? Maybe the young people who are roving the streets of Europe have the right answer: Let's run.

Christianity, however, supplies another answer to Benjamin's "Who am I?"—an answer that does not leave Benjamin simply with the establishment of his individual identity. It goes further and points out that occupational choice is a matter of a person's own moral character. In short, we must deal with two questions: (1) Who is man

and what is his identity? and (2) How does man, having
an identity, relate to work?

Who Is Man?

Man is a curious phenomenon. Man is the only being that
is unable not to question his identity, the only being who
cannot take his identity for granted.

There are two possible ways to answer the question of
identity. Let me put it personally. On the one hand, I can
seek my identity in the order of things in the cosmos
around me. Here I am only one thing among others. I
see only a mass of particulars from which I am unable to
distinguish myself. I am faced with sheer quantity, and
the mass of particulars becomes a threat.

On the other hand, I can deny that a separate identity
is relevant or desirable and seek solace in a unity with all
things. But if I do this, I become a zero. For example, if
I align myself with a mass political movement, I disap-
pear into the crowd. If I align myself with the things of
the universe (as in pantheistic mysticism), I lose all possibility of individuality. If I look for my identity in a pantheistic framework, I find my essential character as a dis-
tinguishable individual denied. Looking for my identity
in the sum total of all other individual things, identifying
myself with everything else, I become, not equal in the
sense of parallel, but unified with everything else and no
longer "there" as an individual. The result is that in both
Hinduism and much of our own culture I soon become
replaceable. That is not a satisfactory answer to the question of my identity.

What I need is a response to my own individuality that
comes from beyond the particular, beyond the material,
beyond the immediate situation. Any definition of the
peculiar individuality of man must come from outside
the present external order. It must have some degree of
objective verifiability which is also open to subjective ver-

15

ification. In other words, it must explain all men and all men's behavior, not in the abstract but in an intimate, subjective form.

For one thing, man finds himself different from the animal. Animals only react to their environment. They do not store information that has no relationship to the present or the possibility of immediate reaction. An animal filters mental impressions that correspond to its organs and reacts to them. Furthermore, an animal has no creativity in the sense of fantasy or imagination. Man, however, is, as we say in German, *weltoffen*, open to creative restructuring of his present environment. He seeks his identity from beyond the immediate. Man acts rather than reacts, and he can be creative and act beyond the immediate reality.

Is this feeling of transcendence an illusion? Is it sheer hypocrisy? Is man attributing something greater to himself than what corresponds to objective reality?

The Bible, it seems to me, gives an answer that corresponds to what man feels and affirms. First, it traces his identity to an origin beyond the present order of existence. It claims that God—a God who is not confined by immediate existence, who is not a part of what is materially there—has made man in his own image (Gen. 1:26). It claims, therefore, that the primary relationship of man is beyond the immediate physical existence of particulars. His primary relationship is to God.

Second, the Bible says that man was placed on earth as God's vice-regent, the one who is to take responsibility over the rest of creation by virtue of the fact that he is made in the image of God.

So out of the ground the LORD God formed every beast of the field and every bird of the air, and brought them to the man to see what he would call them; and whatever the man called every living creature, that was its name. The man gave names to all cattle, and to the birds of the air, and to every beast of the field; but for the man there was not found a helper fit for him. (Gen. 2:19-20)

What we have here is God creating and bringing his creation to man so that man can categorize the environment in which he lives. In Genesis 2:19-20 we have a framework within which the particulars of creation are placed in the proper relationship to man. Man is the one who groups his environment into classes rather than being grouped by his environment into a class—man.

Now how does he perform this classification? It is intriguing that when you look at these two short verses you find that Adam categorized his environment by means of language, of imagination. In a sense, Adam was a scientist. In Hebrew, the name of a person or thing in some way relates to who the person is or what the thing is. Thus the names which Adam gave to the animals indicated what the animals were. Adam dominated, ordered, categorized, shaped the environment in which he lived, gave form to the rest of God's creation. In doing so, he found no one like himself. And God then gave him Eve.

Adam was the vice-regent of God, being primarily related to God because he was made in God's image. Being the vice-regent of God, he classified the plants and gave them particular names, making the objects his own by labeling them. This is not something animals can do.

Imagination is another aspect of man which is his alone. By *imagination* I mean the formation of mental images of objects that are not present to the senses, especially those that were never perceived in their entirety. In other words, imagination is a mental synthesis of new ideas from elements experienced separately. This is a mark of creativity. It is the human capability to go from our own situation into other situations. It is also the basis for fantasy.

Oftentimes people argue that because we can detect

repetitive sounds in monkeys and in porpoises (and especially because porpoises have a brain structure similar to the human brain), man is nothing more than a complicated monkey or porpoise. Some research has revealed that porpoises have sounds for food, for danger and for greeting. And in fact one can train a porpoise to react to the sounds of human language, to English sounds or French sounds and so forth. Wouldn't it be eventually possible, then, for us to discuss abstract matter, say Hegel's philosophy, with porpoises?

I doubt it. Being able to train a porpoise to respond to a fourth, fifth, sixth, even a thousandth sound, does not prove that you can speak with a porpoise or that the porpoise is an inventor of language, a creator of linguistic data. It only proves that you can train a porpoise to react within a larger environment, filtering more impressions in relationship to the organs that he has. But the fact that he can be trained to make one sound or a thousand sounds does not mean that the porpoise is creative. He is not learning a language the way a child learns a language.

One way a child learns language is by putting things in its mouth—because that is very sensitive—and then attaching gurgles and sounds to the objects. The first two stages go smoothly, but in the third stage comes a clash. His parents insist on one sound and the child insists on another. Of course, in the end the parents win, but the child is being creative in the sounds that he makes. By contrast, porpoises throughout the world have a universal sound pattern. An individual porpoise apparently cannot be creative in the sound that it makes.

What distinguishes man from the animal, then, is the possibility of being creative beyond the immediate environment. Man can enlarge his environment, the porpoise cannot.

And man can enlarge his own environment not only in

the things perceived but also in the establishment of relationships between the things perceived and those things which have no objective existence. Fairy tales and fantasies mark man's creativity. They show that man does not just react to his environment but rather acts beyond it, creating things which did not exist before him.

So, when the Bible says that God placed man in the garden and brought all the animals to him and he named them, we have a statement of man's peculiar identity. He is related first of all to God because he is made in the image of God, and that makes him different from all other creation. And next he is the vice-regent of God and able to be creative.

In my daily existence, therefore, the present situation does not need to subject me and stifle me. For the world around me is not the final point of relationship. Life and creativity extend beyond the mere now. It is grounded in that which is beyond even the Greek cosmos (a set situation regulated by a static, platonic heaven which holds in balance all finite particulars of the ordinary world). For even here, there is no possibility for significant change, for going beyond the immediate situation to a future moment or a moment in fantasy, because everything is predetermined and set.

In Christianity, however, and in our own experience, we realize that life is not only in the mere now: Both past and future are real before God. Thus a Christian can have a dynamic view of history, because the future is different from the present and because the future can to some extent be shaped by my creative activity as a significant man. Being a man in part implies the ability to change the future. Man is not subject to his environment, nor does it define him.

Of course there are limits. A man has to eat, he has to walk rather than fly, he has to be at this moment of history rather than that, but he has the creative ability to go beyond his immediate situation.

Take the case of the artist. Michelangelo was limited by the block of marble that he saw in Carrara, but the figure that he sculpted was not what he saw in the quarry. He carved it originally from something in his mind.

The same is true in science. The scientist looks at data, forms a theory, tests it, and, if it fits the situation, goes on to apply it or to see how it relates to something else. He is not just reacting to a present situation. He is able to fashion hypotheses that are not only verifiable but once having been fashioned can then themselves be a part of the reason that the future is different from the past.

Furthermore, from creativity have come what we might call the good elements of the industrial revolution. All our scientific and technological advances, both in what we Germans so nicely call the *inexact* sciences of sociology and anthropology and the *exact* sciences of physics and chemistry, proceed on the basis of man's imaginative and creative ability.

Moreover, only on the basis of this creativity is there a foundation for personal relationships and for enjoying each other. As men we can create rather than react, and this makes possible humanness and community that go beyond mere chemical compatibility.

The Bible rejects any identity that derives from nature or from the immediate environment. The world is not the final integration point, and if we look for it there, we shall only find finite gods and idolatry, as the Greeks did, or dehumanizing jobs and hypocrisy as Benjamin did in *The Graduate*.

What Is the Place of Work?

Nonetheless, when the Bible gives me a place and says who I am and affirms my identity not from the immediate surroundings but rather from God himself, then I come to what is so intimately linked with my identity—

the need to be creative over God's universe. And this is work. Just as God expressed himself and his character in his creation and in his revelation to man, so the image of God in man must be expressed, must be externalized. It is not a threat to me if I work, if my identity is no longer tied to the job that I do, the part in society that I play or the body in nature that I am. In fact, all of a sudden, work and creativity, so intimately linked together, become a challenge.

Many Christians feel that work is a result of the Fall. They remember that when Adam was punished, he had to gain his livelihood by the sweat of his brow, he had to till the ground, do difficult and dangerous work.

For example, Jacques Ellul in "Work and Calling" gives an excellent description of how Christians through Western history have viewed the notion of work. His own view is that "work is of the order of necessity. It is given to man by God as a *means* of survival, but it is also posed as a *condition* for survival. . . . It is not, therefore, a part of the order of grace, of gratuity, of love, of freedom. . . . Like violence, like political power, work also is part of the order of necessity. One cannot escape it: it is the human condition resulting from the rupture with God."[1] Work is not freedom and it has "no ultimate value, no transcendent meaning."[2] As he says, "Work is thus limited in everyday life, and even limited to the banal, to the 'hopeless.' It is neither value nor creation."[3]

To the extent that Ellul rejects the medieval notion that "work is purely and simply a curse, a sign of the condemnation of Adam" he is, I believe, to be commended.[4] But he also rejects the solution posed by Luther. Work, Luther thought, is equally valid before and after the Fall, because "it is a part of the order he [God] established for man."[5] Luther argues that "in making shoes, the cobbler serves God, obeys his calling from God, quite as much as the preacher of the Word."[6]

21

By making a distinction between calling and work, Ellul, however, drives a wedge between the infinite and the finite, between God and man, between the activity that matters to God and the activity that matters to human history. He sees work as "the most completely relative type of situation"[7] and only relevant because it prolongs human history. This view resembles rather remarkably the neo-orthodox division between the absolute and relative, infinite and finite, eternal and temporal, *Geschichte* and *Historie,* applied to calling and work. In any case, Ellul rejects the notion that work can have ultimate significance, that all of reality—sacred and secular—stands in relationship to the infinite-personal God. Ellul asks the question whether his solution is "not in reality a solution of despair" and answers, "To be sure, it contradicts the idea of the Christian life as the unified life, integrating the totality of our action and feelings."[8]

The Bible, it seems to me, is on the side of Luther. In Genesis 2:15 before the Fall we find this statement: "The LORD God took the man and put him in the garden of Eden to till it and keep it." That was creative work. It was not merely a matter of man's survival. It was a part of man's original purpose. It tied in with his being creative and imaginative, with his being God's vice-regent. So it isn't that man did not work before the Fall but that his work had a different character. Before the Fall, work was easy and joyful; afterwards it was toil. But in both cases work is intimately linked with the question of who God is and who man is.

Indeed, we make a mistake if we wander the streets of Europe, fleeing from any kind of work and creativity. We are wrong to seek an answer only to the question of who I am and not to the question of what I shall do.

But if I see work in relationship to creativity, then I no longer work just because everybody else does it or because it is expected of me as a necessity. I do not have to

22

look at it as a burden contrary to myself, nor see myself caught in the utilitarianism and machine likeness of our own age. Rather, I can see work as an extension of my own essential being.

The Bible frequently speaks of outward manifestations of inward reality. If my inward reality is indeed to be a child of God made in the image of God, then I should project who I am out into the external world. I cannot continue in idleness once I have perceived who I am. This point is made repeatedly in the Bible.

Go to the ant, O sluggard;
   consider her ways, and be wise.
Without having any chief,
   officer or ruler,
she prepares her food in summer.
   and gathers her sustenance in harvest.
How long will you lie there, O sluggard?
   When will you arise from your sleep?
A little sleep, a little slumber,
   a little folding of the hands to rest,
and poverty will come upon you like a vagabond,
   and want like an armed man. (Prov. 6:6-11)

If you are a man, work. It is a necessary part of the expression of who you are. It has nothing to do with the Fall or the present society.

Proverbs has much to say about this: "The soul of the sluggard craves, and gets nothing, while the soul of the diligent is richly supplied" (Prov. 13:4). Or: "He who tills his land will have plenty of bread, but he who follows worthless pursuits has no sense" (Prov. 12:11; cf. 28:19). "The sluggard buries his hand in the dish, and will not even bring it back to his mouth" (Prov. 19:24). What a picture of a man who refuses to express who he is!

Do you see a man who is wise in his own eyes?
   There is more hope for a fool than for him.
The sluggard says, "There is a lion in the road!

23

There is a lion in the streets!"
As a door turns on its hinges,
    so does a sluggard on his bed.
The sluggard buries his hand in the dish;
    it wears him out to bring it back to his mouth.
The sluggard is wiser in his own eyes
    than seven men who can answer discreetly.
                                        (Prov. 26:12-16)
The sluggard makes a lot of commotion, but he doesn't
get anywhere. He is like a door that moves but doesn't
move because it's caught on its hinges. The writer of
Ecclesiastes expressed it well: "Through sloth the roof
sinks in, and through indolence the house leaks" (Eccles.
10:18). Nothing happens, nothing gets done, but there
are definite results if you do not accept who you are as a
man and if you do not work.

The New Testament also speaks about sloth. The parable of the talents (Mt. 25:14-30) is a strong indictment of
the "slothful servant" (v. 26). Romans 12:11 reads,
"Never flag in zeal, be aglow with the Spirit, serve the
Lord." But it was apparently in Thessalonica where the
problem was most prevalent, for we find in both of Paul's
letters a charge to work. In 1 Thessalonians we read,
"But we exhort you, brethren, to do so more and more,
to aspire to live quietly, to mind your own affairs, and to
work with your hands, as we charged you; so that you
may command the respect of outsiders, and be dependent on nobody" (1 Thess. 4:10-12). In his second letter,
Paul expands on this:

Now we command you, brethren, in the name of our
Lord Jesus Christ, that you keep away from any brother who is living in idleness and not in accord with the
tradition that you received from us. For you yourselves know how you ought to imitate us; we were not
idle when we were with you, we did not eat any one's
bread without paying, but with toil and labour we

worked night and day, that we might not burden any of you. It was not because we have not that right, but to give you in our conduct an example to imitate. For even when we were with you, we gave you this command: If any one will not work, let him not eat. For we hear that some of you are living in idleness, mere busybodies, not doing any work. Now such persons we command and exhort in the Lord Jesus Christ to do their work in quietness and to earn their own living. (2 Thess. 3:6-12)

And just to show that this isn't a harsh statement and must never be taken as harshness, to show that we must allow the individuality of the situation, Paul adds, "Brethren, do not be weary in well-doing" (v. 13). The balance is there, but the principle is clear. If any man will not work, neither let him eat.

We are called on as Christians to be men before God, to have character, to fulfill the purpose of our creation which is to glorify God by being the ones he has made us to be. All of this is linked with expressing into the external world by the creative activity of work something of our identity as men. Work is linked with man's superior status. He is different from everything else that is there.

Shaping Our Environment

In fact, since we are superior, we are admonished to control our environment lest it control us, as it surely controls the parent generation in *The Graduate*. Of course, controlling, forming and shaping the environment does not mean spoiling it. There must be balance.

Consider, for example, the whole question of ecology. Before we conclude as some have that man ought to keep his hands off the environment because what he has done with it has been destructive, we should look at the actual situations we face. What should I do with the rats that come into my house? If I choose to let the rats live, they

25

will gnaw my baby. The rats will not choose to let my baby sleep. If I choose not to control my environment, my environment will control me. The question with my own chalet in Switzerland is what to do with the wasps that dig a hole right next to it and fly around in our living room. If I do not control my environment creatively, I will be in trouble. It doesn't mean, however, that I have to kill the wasps and rats that are miles from the nearest habitation. Control means establishing a balance.

The same thing, it seems to me, is true in the area of jobs. Unless you shape your work, your work will shape you. I remember a man who came to us some time ago. His wife had accused him of having the engineer's syndrome; all he did was think engineering and play with figures. She wanted to divorce him. And we can feel for her. For the engineer had not managed to control his environment, and his environment had shaped him.

But how can a man shape his environment? What can he do? It seems to me that the first thing one can do—and this is beautiful to watch in children—is to control the environment by language. By means of language man sets up the defining limit and thereby removes the fear of the unknown. This, I think, is one of the reasons why a child attaches particular sounds to particular objects, for suddenly the object becomes known, classified. The child has made the object subject to himself and dependent on himself. He has defined *it*.

Therefore, what is needed is an understanding of our identity in relationship to God. This kind of identity is big enough to keep us from being caught up in our environment; it allows us to express ourselves in the work that we do and it keeps the work from crushing us. If my identity is gone and God is unknown, I no longer know who I am except as a series of subjective experiences. And this is modern man's dilemma, being caught up in the fear of being alone and insignificant in history. The fear of being alone and insignificant is often what prevents creativity in the people around us.

Moreover, modern man easily becomes subject to technology and mass impersonalization. Rather than being free and creative and able to take advantage of a higher technology, man becomes less than a zero. And yet at the price of being more primitive, he can be more man. So what shall we choose?

We live in a crazy age. The principle of success has become so important that anything that leads to it seems morally right. But this twists man and denies his essential humanity. If I try for success at the cost of being man, what have I gained? Benjamin indeed is right to refuse to work when his father cannot give him the answer to his identity. When the job is more important than the humanity of the worker, our society is sick.

In the last few years in a few factories throughout the world, I am thinking specifically of a Swedish automobile factory, there has been a reorganization of the way in which the cars are made. They used to be made on an assembly line, each man doing one task over and over again and never seeing the results of his labor. Now the factory is organized into groups of ten men who make a portion of a car from beginning to end and then start all over again and make another one. This is a more humane way of working. It gives a sense of creativity because the thing created is immediately seen as it takes shape under the hands of the worker.

It is ironic that the notion of incentive, which seems to be a rather American, even capitalist, notion, is on a very personal level more wisely applied in the backyards in Russia than in the United States. Many Russians are able to keep a pig or to grow a few vegetables. These then are their own and can be bought and sold. In America, and in much of Europe, incentive is linked only to an increase of money.

27

Creativity and Craftsmanship

What we as Christians should really be interested in is the idea of craftsmanship. We should surround ourselves with things that have been made by men so that we see the link between the creativity of man and the thing that he produces. We should emphasize the products that come from the hands of men. There is surely no craftsmanship in a man's doing nothing but tightening bolts on a wheel.

I recently came across a record of folk music that was made in Villars, an alpine village in Switzerland. The album pictures five men, a medical doctor, a mailman, a farmer and two railroad employees. These five men had formed a musical group. They were craftsmen—amateur craftsmen—whose product was the result of genuine creativity. In wide areas of Europe we still have the concept that man counts more than the work that he does or the education that he has, that man himself is of greater importance. His craftsmanship and his creativity express his worth.

A friend of mine who is an American engineer and builds bridges lost his job in his father's company because of the way he tried to solve a personnel problem. What he found was that the workers would come, dig ditches for bridges for a month and then get so bored that they would leave. There was a tremendous turnover. So my friend thought that as a Christian he ought to do something about it. He hatched an idea. He decided to travel across Europe and photograph Roman bridges that had been built 2,000 years ago and that still stand. He took the pictures back to the ditchdiggers and said, "Look, here's what you're building, a bridge. And how long it will stand depends on the way you dig the ditch. Your craftsmanship is involved."

But his father said that that was no job for a vice-president, and he fired him. It's inefficient. Flying to Europe to take pictures of bridges! Use the men to dig the ditches instead of showing them how to be human and how to be creative. Nevertheless, as a result of these pictures, the ditchdiggers began to say to themselves, "We're building bridges. And if we build them well, they'll stand for 2,000 years." And they began to work better, and after a couple of months some of them moved up to the next higher level and then to the next higher level, and the turnover was much, much less. For here was a humane situation in which the individual was encouraged to be creative.

Very often when people come to L'Abri and are really hung up about what they should do, when they feel the total sociological pressure that after graduation from high school they must go to college, we often encourage them to become craftsmen. We suggest they become, say, sandal-makers in Greenwich Village or candle-makers or carpenters. We encourage them to work with their hands so that their craftsmanship can be felt and so that their work will not just be a contribution to a big object, where the identity of the individual is destroyed because there is no relationship between the creative process in the mind and what is expressed through the hands. Sometimes taking a little job can help a person feel his own importance, his own individuality, his own character. For if the relationship between our creativity in our mind and that which we create with our hands is gone, then we become discouraged from being creative.

Do you have trouble in the area of work and identity? Then begin with little things, little things you can manage, little things you can see. Become a worker in the street department and prune bushes along the street as one student did who came to live near us. In the evening, he came back and said, "Without my creativity in clipping bushes, that street would still have bushes hanging over the edge." You might say that that's not very beautiful and not very stimulating, but to the person who has a profound question about whether he has any importance at all in modern society, it matters. One doesn't have to clip bushes all the rest of his life, but he begins with little things.

Another thing we do as people come to live with us is not really done deliberately, for it is part of the normal running of a home. Everyone who comes as a student is asked to help clean the lavatories. And it doesn't matter who comes. It is interesting to watch the reactions of various people. Those who really know who they are hardly mind at all, for they realize that cleaning the lavatory doesn't identify them. But a lot of people feel that they are identified by the work they do, so they resent the task, and that has sad results.

It is of primary importance to get your identity straightened out. But at the same time, we can say that having an identity begins with expressing it in little ways, doing insignificant things but things you can see, things that show you have done something that has really changed what was there. Identity is truly tied up with creativity, and creativity with expression, and expression with work.

Second, I encourage those who are concerned about their identity to work with their hands and to get the feel of dominion over the stuff that surrounds them. Learn from the hippie: He walks barefoot over the ground and the mud comes up between his toes. He is much closer to what is there than we are. If he has a Hindu mentality, then he is identifying with the mud, and that is not what I am talking about. But if he has something of the external world in his hands and if he shapes it and has control over it, then he is truly expressing his dominion as man made in the image of God. There is something beautiful about feeling the things you work with, something beautiful about being a carpenter and feeling the grain of the wood and being sensitive to the kind of wood you have and the kind of knife you can use on it.

In a discussion group we were once talking about the need to express Christianity into the external world. We noted that being spiritual is not just speaking about Christ but also being the people we are supposed to be in relationship to God and to the total reality of our bodies and minds. One of the Christians objected to this. And a non-Christian said, "Why, Paul took time to make tents." And then he added, "If anyone ever found a piece of one of Paul's tents, it had better be beautifully made." And he's right. Work with your hands and do things well.

Third, I would encourage all of us to work with the things that reflect human creativity directly so that if possible we do not find ourselves in a job that requires us to do nothing but, say, fabricate cement blocks, the identity of which we do not recognize in the houses that are constructed, where there is no continuity between our creative expression and the result. It won't go. It will give us a feeling of insignificance.

Of course, there are jobs that are so routine and so mechanical that they tend to reduce the worker to a machine and to eliminate any possibility for creativity. Some of these are necessary in any society. But if a man is to live in the full circumference of life, he can deliberately search for situations beyond the immediate task for the expression of his creativity. For example, if one has a job on an assembly line and he can't get the foreman to allow creativity on the job, he cannot only use the coffee breaks but also the after-work hours to express himself and to be human by choice. Creativity starts not in getting coffee from the automat but in talking to the people with you in the queue. It extends to friendship and to the relationship to your family and possibly any number of avocations. In a fallen world, not everything we do can be creative, but much can, and we should make every effort to find those situations.

Money, Time and Leisure

I would mention a fourth area which might seem strange at first. We live in an age of checks and credit cards and very little cash. What does this do to us? It removes us from the immediacy of the value of money, and that removes us in a real sense from the reality of work and the value of creative action. When you never see what you make and you only have a figure on a piece of paper, you may well feel that you have not been paid. It is not that you can't pay your bills, because there is something in your bank account. But you don't get the feeling that the money is yours.

My wife Debby had this sensation when she worked. Seventeen percent or so went to tax, and she never saw it. The only way she overcame the discouragement was to regard the tax as a part of what she didn't earn and thus to keep from thinking this seventeen percent was a part of her salary. During this time our car broke down and we had to have it repaired on credit. Debby went through the strange emotion that the payments on a car were something she never possessed. It wasn't real.

Some of you may not feel this way, but this reaction is not farfetched. There are many in our culture who buy everything on the installment plan and who get so much in debt that they owe more in monthly payments than they earn in a month. So they take a second routine job and the possibility for creativity is even less.

Fifth, as Christians we must understand that work and creativity do not necessarily imply an immediate result. In the larger Christian framework, *who* man is guarantees that his actions will be significant to the extent that sometime in the future there will be a real change. But we do not always see that immediately. Our age makes history a zero. Men live only for the day. That stifles creativity because so often results are not immediate. In the Christian framework we live not only in the present but also in the continuity of time, because God is there and knows the end from the beginning. Creativity is even there when the result takes twenty years in coming. But man's identity comes from outside the mere present. So, as a person gets a firmer and firmer grasp on who he is, he can see his own creativity in a larger framework and can work even when he does not see the results.

A sixth area with which we should be concerned is leisure. We must also "work" in our time off; recreation implies activity and not entertainment only. We have found a real change in the people who have come to L'Abri over the years. Eleven years or so ago, rarely did anyone on his day off go down to the pub and watch television. Rarely did people go to Lausanne to be entertained and have a meal and come back. Rather, we took walks along the Panex Road, the only flat road near us in the mountains. We went on hikes after our discussions and chatted and enjoyed ourselves. There was a greater sense of creativity then, for now more and more people are looking for entertainment instead of creating entertainment for themselves. We should seek refreshment through playing, imagining, telling stories, digging in the garden, even cleaning lavatories.

Often when people come to L'Abri and listen to the lectures, participate in the discussions and conversations, it becomes an entertainment, something that is carried into them from the outside. They write it down and go home with three pounds of notes and think they have the world's answers in their pocket. Then all of a sudden comes the collapse.

If you have never learned to creatively understand by establishing new relationships among the data that you hear (and hopefully check), you can fall flat on your face. We must express who we are and the reality of who God is in all of the things that we do and think about.

33

Wind-up Men

We can see the need for creativity in yet another area. It seems to me that fifteen years ago, say, children were raised in such a fashion as to foster initiative and imagination. Debby and I and our children have talked about this recently, and we wonder whether children today are allowed to develop imagination and create situations by themselves. With talking dolls and wind-up cars and television, children no longer need to create; everything is supplied. And where everything is supplied, imagination and creativity die.

A little girl who plays with her dolls that don't talk has a wide variety of imaginative situations, but get her a wind-up doll that has four sentences and her imagination starts only when the doll breaks down. I think one of the worst things you can do is to give a child a wind-up, talking doll.

God does not treat us that way. He does not put us in a box, but into an environment over which we can be creative. He doesn't put us in a spiritual box either. He wants us to develop character and holiness by choice and creativity in relationship to who God is. Our first products may not be very good. They may even be ugly. But we have to start where we are.

I remember a young man who was schizophrenic. He would carry on conversations with himself. "Bill," part of him would say, "They're going to get you, they're going to get you." And the other Bill would say, "I'm going to resist, I'm going to resist, I'm going to resist." From a background where his father worked and his work was his identity, Bill was going to resist a nine-to-five job. He was not going to work because that was not a sufficient identity. He said, "I'm not going to work. I'm going to write poetry."

His father kept writing to us, saying, "When is he coming back to finish college? What's wrong with the

boy? Do you think he'll ever fit into society?" And Bill
would say, "They're going to get you. But I'm not going
to be gotten." This was very real to him.

He was at L'Abri for three months, became a Chris-
tian, went to England, worked with schizophrenics with
R. D. Laing, came back to L'Abri and then went home to
America.

He lived with his parents, saw his father still doing his
nine-to-five work, and Bill said, "They're not going to get
me." And he sat home for a month. Slowly—he didn't
follow his father, not in that kind of identity—he took a
job from 6:30 in the morning until 4:30 in the afternoon.
Then he found that he could have lunch with his wife
and they could have a half hour to enjoy each other.
Then he would go back to work, do an hour's overtime,
go home, have a two-hour nap and read. In fact, he read
for three or four hours every day.

You know what his job was? His job was to sort out and
polish brass bathroom fixtures. For any thinking person,
that seems awful. But not for Bill, not once he had really
become a Christian and had seen that there was no need
to be shaped by his job. In the middle of his work and
the rest of the day, he could be creative. He wrote us a
letter, saying that it was such a good feeling to be working
and to be expressing himself as a person.

You don't have to work for society or fit into a mold,
but you must work for yourself in order to be real, in
order to be a man whom God has made in his own image,
in order to live in the reality which exists. Only then can
you be where Bill was at that point—free to be a man
made in the image of God.

From the spiritual point of view, work is a matter of
being, of character, of what makes man man. It is not a
matter of what society demands. Your identity, unless
you work, is merely a theoretical identity, for you must
manifest it, you must externalize it, lest the theory just

collapse and you become a zero. If the theoretical is not verifiable in the external world and the work you do as a creative being, your identity will lose its reality. To be a vice-regent of God over God's creation means to work creatively and to enjoy it.

An essay in *Time* magazine asks, "Is the work ethic going out of style?"[9] Four challenges to the work ethic (the notion that work is valuable in itself) are listed: early retirement, absenteeism, refusing overtime work and refusing to hold menial jobs. These challenges are explained by increasing affluence, the new rise in hedonism and antimaterialist notions of the counter culture. Whether or not these challenges mean that America has lost the work ethic is then answered by statistics that show that ninety percent of the male work force is actually working, the same percentage as twenty-five years ago. But the question of man's relationship to his work and the worker's satisfaction in creativity is not even asked.

A Christian understands that only in creative activity do we externalize the identity we have as men made in the image of God. This, then, is the true basis for work.

Creativity
and the
Value
of Property

"Property rights ... exist.
... But what is really
protected is man's creative
mental activity—his ideas
which are externalized into
things which he owns
and has a right to possess
and enjoy."

2

In 1848, Karl Marx in the *Communist Manifesto* cried out against private property because he saw how capitalism had exploited men. He saw the abuses of child labor and of poor wages. Today the cry is no longer against private property (on the basis of the misuse of capitalism) but rather against anything private—property, life or human individuality.

In the light of a rapidly changing world in which the facade of privacy and private property brings out the hypocrisy and selfishness of man, the abolition of private property cannot create a human community. Someone will have to bring order out of the ensuing chaos of conflicting claims, and whoever does this is likely to destroy whatever is otherwise left of the privacy of the individual.

When law and structure are gone, tyranny follows. Might alone dictates right. The slaveries of our own age —the slaveries of body and mind, the slaveries of the political right and the political left—are past reminders and threatening prophecies of the future.

If we are to speak the gospel into such a situation as this, what is needed? How does the good news apply to the present life of the Christian?

I believe that what we need is a renewed balance between form and freedom, in this case a balance between property and community, between individual rights and compassion for others. Such a balance is only possible under a God who is both holy and loving, a God who himself is law and has property because he is personal and creates, but who also is compassionate and loves and shares abundantly that which he has. Only the God of the Bible can give a true definition of the relationship between the polarities—between property and communion, between rights and compassion.

Property and Creativity

Scripture points out that property is intimately tied to creatorship. The creator owns that which he has created: "The earth is the LORD's and the fullness thereof, the world and those who dwell therein" (Ps. 24:1). God owns the world, he is its creator. Another psalm expresses the same idea in a different context—the notion that the Jewish nation could approach God by fulfilling the law legalistically. The Pharisees felt that men could establish a relationship with God through a series of sacrifices offered self-righteously. But God says this will not do:

I will accept no bull from your house,
    nor he-goat from your folds.
For every beast of the forest is mine,
    the cattle on a thousand hills.
I know all the birds of the air,
    and all that moves in the field is mine.
If I were hungry, I would not tell you;
    for the world and all that is in it is mine. (Ps. 50:9-12)

God, as the Creator, is the proprietor of the earth. We cannot, therefore, come to God with something which is already his and succeed in pleasing him.

We might note in passing that the Bible never pictures

animals as creators or owners of property; as far as we know they have no capacity to create, no ability to imagine or to externalize what they imagine even if they could imagine. Thus animals can *own* nothing.

On the other hand, the Bible emphasizes that man, like God, is a creator. Man too has rights that extend to the things that he has made. They originate in his creative activity. He has put, as it were, his stamp upon them. They are his property.

The Ten Commandments, especially in those laws that govern property, bear this out: "You shall not steal" and "You shall not covet" (Ex. 20:15 and 17). The latter is given specificity, for one shouldn't covet his neighbor's house, wife, servants, animals or "anything" that is his neighbor's.

The laws that cover property presuppose property rights. You shall not steal because what you steal belongs to somebody else. And if it belongs to him, it is his to use, and the enjoyment and the fruits of its use are his as well.

Two of Jesus' parables likewise affirm the value of property: the parable of the talents (Mt. 25:14-30) and the parable of the unjust steward (Lk. 16:1-13). The latter is especially important for there we are told that men are the stewards of the property they receive from God as a natural outflow of their own creativity. That the steward deals unjustly is not the point of the parable. Rather Christ is speaking to the Christian to work now in such a fashion that after the Christian's own death there will be significant results. For the steward, even though unjustly, creatively affected events which took place after his dismissal from stewardship.

Property rights, therefore, exist in Scripture. But what is really protected is man's creative mental activity—his ideas which are externalized into things which he owns and has a right to possess and to enjoy. Property includes both the tangibles and the intangibles, things as well as ideas.

Moreover, true communion and true community are based on property rights. For unless a person owns something he can share, there can be no community. Social justice in the community at large and real sharing in smaller groups are both based on that principle.

As Christians speaking the gospel into the world today, we must never forget this: The right to own property is presupposed in Scripture, and it is established on the ground that man is a creator. This becomes the basis for our struggle as Christians against social injustice.

Property and Justice

There is a growing danger today that by enactment and execution of social legislation society will be pulled into an uncreative redistribution of wealth. Law was once understood to be a description of the boundaries within which human relationships should take place. But for our generation it has become a naked sword expressing the heightened selfishness of every man for himself. In this way, law as it is increasingly used is destroying man. We used to believe that the life of man depends on men living in justice with each other. Now we have only an extended series of clashes in which all social relationships end.

The wealthy, on the one hand, keep their wealth and disregard the pressing needs and the social injustice around them. They achieve their identity from the property they hold. The poor, on the other hand, demand economic relief instead of giving thought to their own creative possibilities. Their demand for support becomes their identity. For both rich and poor, objects bind men together and take the place of real human relationships.

Many who have made real contributions have had their creativity destroyed because their rights over what they have created have been violated. The work of their hands has been taken from them. On the other hand, those who have received the property of others have had their own creativity destroyed because they no longer are required to search for ways to support themselves. The necessity for creativity has been removed.

Justice is a prime category throughout Scripture. It is rooted in God's existence and character. God has always pressed for justice, perfectly. The Christian church and individual Christians, however, have pressed for justice only imperfectly. For example, the Old Testament reveals that God desires men (both individually and collectively) to protect and take care of the widows and the orphans (Ex. 22:22-24; Deut. 14:28-29). The model is that God is there; he will take care of those who have not. A true communion must, therefore, be expressed.

The command not to steal, which states so strongly that property does exist, applies not just to outright theft but to other ways of gaining wealth. The rich man too can steal in the ways he gains his wealth.

Look, for instance, at one practical application of the law of God in an individual situation: "You shall not oppress a hired servant who is poor and needy, whether he is one of your brethren or one of the sojourners who are in your land within your towns" (Deut. 24:14). Jew or Gentile, one of your brothers of any race or nationality or a stranger at your door—he is not to be oppressed. The text does not leave *oppression* an empty word: "You shall give him his hire on the day he earns it, before the sun goes down (for he is poor, and sets his heart upon it); lest he cry against you to the LORD, and it be sin in you" (v. 15). So, if a poor man is working with you in a wage relationship, a contractual relationship, you must pay him when he has finished his work. If not, he will cry to the Lord because he depends so much on what he has earned. It is his property and you must not withhold it

43

from him.

The same charge is repeated in James 5:1-6:

Come now, you rich, weep and howl for the miseries that are coming upon you. Your riches have rotted and your garments are moth-eaten. Your gold and silver have rusted, and their rust will be evidence against you and will eat your flesh like fire. You have laid up treasure for the last days. Behold, the wages of the labourers who mowed your fields, which you kept back by fraud, cry out; and the cries of the harvesters have reached the ears of the Lord of hosts. You have lived on the earth in luxury and in pleasure; you have fattened your hearts in a day of slaughter. You have condemned, you have killed the righteous man; he does not resist you.

The poor are simply too poor to fight back. Notice that James does not speak against wealth as such but against wealth earned by corruption, the wealth that comes by not paying a man at the end of his work, by making him wait, by keeping the money in the bank and heaping up interest. This is a strong statement against all social injustice. The same charge extends to any inequitable handling of salary, paying people of one social class or sex more or less depending on whether or not they are in a position to protest effectively. Stealing includes any accumulation of wealth by unjust tactics.

But there is another side to the issue. While the Bible emphasizes the reality of property, it also teaches that one person's creative activity is to be qualified by other people's creative activity. Creativity is to be mutually stimulating. In other words, we are not to take away from those who have and give to those who have not, but rather to stimulate those who do not have to outcreate those who have. For those who have often become sleepy in their wealth. And those who have not may well outcreate them. Of course, this takes time and patience, determi-

44

nation and love, and a real understanding of the world around us. But if one has outcreated the sleepy, he has done well.

The cry for social equality offered up today is usually void of any such concept. It is characterized by a lack of creativity and often even an unwillingness to try to be creative. Instant equality of social condition is the goal. The affirmation of mannishness and creativity is not even considered. It is not that one ought to outcreate someone else in order to be better than he is. Not in the least. But God has created a universe in which much is to be enjoyed and he has made this "wealth" available to those who are creative.

This idea is not at all new. Paul mentions it in both his letters to the church at Thessalonica. We have quoted these passages in the previous chapter, but they bear repeating here. Sloth must have been a real problem, for Paul writes:

> But concerning love of the brethren you have no need to have any one write to you, for you yourselves have been taught by God to love one another; and indeed you do love all the brethren throughout Macedonia. But we exhort you, brethren, to do so more and more, to aspire to live quietly, to mind your own affairs, and to work with your hands, as we charged you; so that you may command the respect of outsiders, and be dependent on nobody. (1 Thess. 4:9-12)

In his second letter, Paul uses even stronger language:

> For even when we were with you, we gave you this command: If any one will not work, let him not eat. For we hear that some of you are living in idleness, mere busybodies, not doing any work. Now such persons we command and exhort in the Lord Jesus Christ to do their work in quietness and to earn their own living. (2 Thess. 3:10-12)

We must understand today's mentality. Things are so

45

easily come by that many have lost the concept of work and creativity over a period of history. Even many Christians think of work as basically evil and deny its value. But notice the logical outcome of such a view: If it becomes our general outlook that even if a man does not work he will nevertheless live on the basis of the wealth of those who do work, then man as a creative agent dies. Paul says, if a person does not work, he should not eat. If he does not work, he has no property. Let him live without property, let him live without bread. When bread comes by free distribution, then man really dies.

Yet this notion permeates our culture. It is in many young people with whom we are confronted in our work and who live on a day-by-day basis. Actually, it is the expression of a shortcut mentality. The idea is that one's daily problems are to be solved by others rather than by one's own activity—thinking and praying, going on your knees and spending time with the Lord and asking for creativity, asking him for a job, a way out of a tough situation you find yourself in even though it may take the next thirty years. People are not so much overcome by their present problems as by the fact that they do not think them through and pray them through. People feel that it is worthless to anticipate a solution that may take thirty years in coming. That's too long! But it isn't—not in God's world where this is the only way to show that we are creative over our situation.

"If Christ comes back tomorrow," as Luther said, "I will plant a tree today." Life will go on until then. The concept that property is a right and that it has to be earned is intimately related to the fact that you have a neignbor whose property is his. There is no instant fulfillment—ever.

It is important for us to emphasize this, for so much in our age is contrary to it. Fly now and pay later, buy on the installment plan, demand instant fulfillment in marriage, expect instant friendship with someone and if it doesn't go, move on the the next person, begin a job and if it doesn't turn out perfectly walk off and leave all your tools. We even expect instant spirituality. But this mentality is sick. Isn't it obvious: If we do not fulfill the purpose for which we were made, if we do not fill out the form in which God created us, our life will be empty. What a hollow feeling to go from one job to another and never create something within the job we have!

The Limitations of Property

The concept of property and property rights can, of course, lead to a great deal of injustice. But God has not left us without some very careful limitations to prevent us from turning the affirmation of property into something harsh and inhuman. These limitations set a balance.

First, we are to be *content* with what we have. Paul writes to Timothy: "There is great gain in godliness with contentment; for we brought nothing into the world, and we cannot take anything out of the world; but if we have food and clothing, with these we shall be content" (1 Tim. 6:6-8). The Greek word translated here as *content* means sufficient, and the work translated as *godliness* is piety, in a good sense, namely, true faith in the God of the Bible. What Paul is saying, then, is that to be content with the things that we do have is indeed to be godly. The understanding of the existence of God and of God's goodness brings this contentment, the realization that what we have is really sufficient.

Our feeling of sufficiency rests on the existence of God and on our relationship to him—a relationship of trust. We trust that he will not fail us, we trust that he will give us enough, we trust that he will give us a creativity where it is lacking, we trust that he will give us bread in some other way if for some reason we cannot work. It is in this context—not that of fatalism or idolatry—that the

47

reasonableness of our contentment lies. We are to be content with what we have and to aspire to more only on the basis of the natural outflow of our creative activity.

A second limitation to the concept of property rights is that we are sojourners in this world. The world is God's and we are stewards of the things he has given us. Furthermore, our true reward, our true wealth, is really God himself and not the *things* he has given us or the things that we make. This was the lesson God taught Abraham: "Fear not, Abram, I am your shield; your reward shall be very great" (Gen. 15:1). What I have to be creative over is held in stewardship to God. Notice too that in 2 Chronicles when Solomon prayed to God he did not ask for wealth but rather for "wisdom and knowledge" (2 Chron. 1:10). And God then replied that because he did not ask for riches or honor but rather for wisdom and knowledge, he would receive not only wisdom and knowledge but riches and honor as well.

Scripture places a third limitation on the concept of property. Paul writes: "But those who desire to be rich fall into temptation, into a snare, into many senseless and hurtful desires that plunge men into ruin and destruction" (1 Tim. 6:9). What Paul is warning against is the danger that lies in our attitude to the wealth we acquire. To be rich is fatal to contentment if we desire to be rich, if that is the whole basis for our creative activity. Paul did not say that it was necessary to throw away our property or to prevent the increase of wealth. Rather he said that we are not to *trust* wealth (cf. Ps. 62). The difference is important.

Furthermore, we are not to make wealth the goal of our work. To have one's total existence wrapped up solely in the acquisition of money or the increase of property is idolatry. It is to put as the object of one's existence not the Creator but the created. Scripture speaks strongly against this. Proverbs 28:20, Ephesians 5:3 and Colos-

sians 3:5, for example, make clear that there should be
no covetousness in the church of Christ.

The passage which overwhelms me, however, is Proverbs 13:7-8:

One man pretends to be rich, yet has nothing;
another pretends to be poor, yet has great wealth.
The ransom of a man's life is his wealth,
but a poor man has no means of redemption.

What the writer of Proverbs is saying is this: When you
are rich you lose your importance as a man. People look
only at your riches and not at you. The rich man is
judged by his wealth; the poor man is judged by who he
is. The poor man hears no voice threatening in the night-
time; no one comes to get him for a ransom. But the rich
man becomes a zero. All that matters is his money.

A fourth limitation that God gives to property and
property rights is very practical. It has to do with balance
in the Christian life and is parallel to other injunctions in
the New Testament. (For example, children are to honor
their parents and to love them; and parents are not to in-
cite their children to wrath. A wife should be subject to
her husband; and a husband should love his wife as
Christ loved the church.) God is concerned for the practical care of his people and balance is thus important.

In Exodus 22, immediately after the giving of the Ten
Commandments, we read:

If you lend money to any of my people with you who is
poor, you shall not be to him as a creditor, and you
shall not exact interest from him. If ever you take your
neighbour's garment in pledge, you shall restore it to
him before the sun goes down; for that is his only cov-
ering, it is his mantle for his body; in what else shall he
sleep? And if he cries to me, I will hear, for I am compassionate. (Ex. 22:25-27)

The teaching is clear. If someone borrows money from
you and, because he is poor, pledges his only garment,

you must return it to him by nightfall lest he freeze. You do not have the right to keep the garment at the expense of compassion.

The same should be true in our own society. We must set limits on the creditor so that basic human existence and that which is necessarily connected with it in the realm of material things is untouchable by the creditor. This is considered in modern bankruptcy procedures, but it must be our personal mentality in practice in all situations in which we are creditors.

Exodus 23 deals with another very practical situation:

For six years you shall sow your land and gather in its yield; but the seventh year you shall let it rest and lie fallow, that the poor of your people may eat; and what they leave the wild beasts may eat. You shall do likewise with your vineyard, and with your olive orchard.

Six days you shall do your work, but on the seventh day you shall rest; that your ox and your ass may have rest, and the son of your bondmaid, and the alien, may be refreshed. (Ex. 23:10-12)

Notice the careful economy. Those who have property may use it, but only within the limitation of the surrounding community. Again it is not enough to make such provisions in statements of law if we ourselves have no corresponding mentality as we live out our lives. Among my friends the principle was carried out by some who gave the first fruits of their garden to the poor of the community in the real desire to share what they had received.

A further illustration of this concept is contained in Leviticus 25:

The land shall not be sold in perpetuity, for the land is mine; for you are strangers and sojourners with me. And in all the country you possess, you shall grant a redemption of the land.

If your brother becomes poor, and sells part of his

50

property, then his next of kin shall come and redeem what his brother has sold. If a man has no one to redeem it, and then himself becomes prosperous and finds sufficient means to redeem it, let him reckon the years since he sold it and pay back the overpayment to the man to whom he sold it; and he shall return to his property. But if he has not sufficient means to get it back for himself, then what he sold shall remain in the hand of him who bought it until the year of jubilee; in the jubilee it shall be released, and he shall return to his property. (Lev. 25:23-28)

What lies behind this set of commands is that the land of Israel was divided among the twelve tribes, every family having a piece. This passage makes clear that no family could ever permanently get rid of their land. They could, however, sell it for up to forty-nine years, but then it would fall back to the family. Apparently, the idea behind the law was to prevent serious exploitation. Property could be bought and sold—but only within certain limitations to provide balance and to preserve human dignity.

Leviticus 19 contains a limitation involving the relationship between the rich and the poor. The property owners are told:

When you reap the harvest of your land, you shall not reap your field to its very border, neither shall you gather the gleanings after your harvest. And you shall not strip your vineyard bare, neither shall you gather the fallen grapes of your vineyard; you shall leave them for the poor and for the sojourner: I am the LORD your God. (Lev. 19:9-10)

In other words, if you are a property owner, you have the right to harvest your field. But there is a limitation involving the community of the people of God: The poor are to partake of the wealth of the rich.

There is a beautiful, practical application of this in the

51

story of Ruth. Boaz, you will recall, commanded his men not only to let Ruth glean along the edges but to let her glean "even among the sheaves" and to "also pull out some from the bundles" on purpose for her (Ruth 2:15-16). Indeed, God affirms the right of property, but he sets a limitation to it in order to provide for those who have not.

Deuteronomy 15 takes up the subject of servants and masters. To the masters, the law says:

Take heed lest there be a base thought in your heart, and you say, "The seventh year, the year of release is near," and your eye be hostile to your poor brother, and you give him nothing, and he cry to the LORD against you, and it be sin in you.

If your brother, a Hebrew man, or a Hebrew woman, is sold to you, he shall serve you six years, and in the seventh year you shall let him go free from you. (Deut. 15:9, 12)

The point here is that a man is not to be a slave forever. There is a limitation to how long a man can be compelled to serve. But not only that:

And when you let him go free from you, you shall not let him go empty-handed; you shall furnish him liberally out of your flock, out of your threshing floor, and out of your wine press; as the LORD your God has blessed you, you shall give to him. (Deut. 15:13-14)

A portion of the riches you have earned from the blessings of the Lord should go to the man who has helped you, even though he has sold his body—his labor—to you for six years running.

The New Testament Balance
Throughout the Old Testament, the limitations on property and property rights are based on the notion of the community of the people of God, the nation of Israel. In the New Testament, the limitations are seen in terms of

the church as well as in the terms of the total human community. Paul expresses this in 2 Thessalonians when he says that if a man does not work, then he should not eat either, but he adds something I have deliberately not mentioned in this chapter until now: "Brethren, do not be weary in well-doing" (2 Thess. 3:13). In other words, "If anyone will not work, neither let him eat, but you, Christians, don't you be weary in well-doing."

Do not be weary in well-doing: This is the limitation of community that God stresses to oppose the wedges wealth drives between all strata of society. It brings back the proper balance in which man is no longer only a means of production but a full-fledged human being and treated as such. Indeed there are wealth and property, but the individual in the community of men and specifically in the community of the church is to be treated as a man.

Brethren, do not be weary in well-doing: This expresses justice before God and the equality of all men, but it allows for the inegality of property and creativity. It does not deny property rights or the legal relationship that exists between a man who has made something and the thing that he has made. Rather property and property rights are seen in relation to the personal contacts between one man and another which are possible only in the framework of the legal.

If we take to heart the fact that we must speak the gospel into our age, then these notions must never remain academic. We must rather actively express their real moral force in a world which is collapsing as a result of its denial of God. The early church practiced such community. They were bound together in the reality of the salvation in Christ Jesus and in the reality of community under the leading of the Holy Spirit.

Notice the description of the first church:
And fear came upon every soul; and many wonders

and signs were done through the apostles. And all who believed were together and had all things in common; and they sold their possessions and goods and distributed them to all, as any had need. And day by day, attending the temple together and breaking bread in their homes, they partook of food with glad and generous hearts, praising God and having favour with all the people. And the Lord added to their number day by day those who were being saved. (Acts 2:43-47)

Or consider this description:

Now the company of those who believed were of one heart and soul, and no one said that any of the things which he possessed was his own, but they had everything in common. And with great power the apostles gave their testimony to the resurrection of the Lord Jesus, and great grace was upon them all. (Acts 4:32-33)

What this shows is that individual property was used for all as they had need. It was not just thrown together and distributed equally. Equal distribution is not the point, not if you stress the individuality of the individual, the mannishness of each man and the creativity of each creator. Rather property was distributed as every man had need.

Furthermore, it was a voluntary communion in which individual needs were considered and met. This is shown in Acts 5 where Peter confronts Ananias and Sapphira with their dishonesty. Peter says, in effect, "You owned land, didn't you? Well, even when you sold it the money was yours and you had a right to use it in any way you wanted to. But to say the part that you gave was all that you got when you sold was wrong. It was not wrong to hold back some of it; it was wrong to lie." Thus, we have in the early church an example of one who has property but does not use it voluntarily or obey God's command for love and communion.

Paul gives further instructions on the use of riches in his first letter to Timothy:

As for the rich in this world, charge them not to be haughty, nor to set their hopes on uncertain riches but on God who richly furnishes us with everything to enjoy. They are to do good, to be rich in good deeds, liberal and generous, thus laying up for themselves a good foundation for the future, so that they may take hold of the life which is life indeed. (1 Tim. 6:17-19)

Paul makes three points. First, the rich are admonished not to be highminded just because they are wealthy. They are not to think of themselves as better than those who are poor, for they are no more nor less man than those who have less. Second, the rich are told not to trust in riches, for that is to trust in something which is made, it is to trust in something which is a part of God's creation and that is idolatry. The rich are to trust in God, the Maker himself. Third, the rich are to be rich in good works, that is, wealthy in man-to-man relationships.

Scripture stresses that property is real. Some men have and some have not. But those who have and those who have not are equally men, and they are to show this equality in the way they love each other. The early church practiced this from Sunday to Sunday, from day to day, a meeting of the rich and the poor in a congregation of the church of Christ on the footing of equality.

This situation is pictured well in 1 Corinthians 11 where the Lord's Supper is seen as a part of "the love feast" where the church sat together and ate together. And if they did this every day, as it seems they did for a while, then what is meant is that the rich shared their food with the poor and the poor had at least one good meal a day. They met because there was equality on the human level even in the midst of inequality on the level of possessions.

55

It was not that the rich bought food and distributed it to the houses of the poor, but that all of them really shared with each other as equals. They sat shoulder to shoulder and talked about things of mutual interest, discussing their problems and praying together. Here was total equality in the humanness of a redeemed community. The rich did not just pay for the poor but they ate the same food as the poor and the poor ate the same food as the rich. They indeed had all things in common.

But there is an important distinction. The rich are commanded to be rich in good works. The poor are admonished to work or not eat. In other words, the command to be rich in good works is a command to the rich but not a claim which the poor can demand from the rich. It is here where community is to start.

Restoring the Balance Today

As Christians we must speak the Christian gospel into the context of a wide history, showing forth the fact that eternal life begins when a person accepts Christ as his Savior. We must show that this new life makes a difference in our own lives, in the life of the surrounding community and in the life of the people of God. But with all our crying *against* social injustice and *for* community, we must understand that community requires that there be something to share. Our first task, therefore, is to begin where Scripture begins—to affirm property and ownership and to affirm thereby the creativity and basic mannishness of man.

L'Abri, for example, is not a school but a community which, in spite of all its imperfections, tries to speak for the reality of God's existence and the reality of his creation. But it cannot do so if property disappears. The community must be something in itself and have something before anything can be shared.

Therefore, while we try to undo social injustice, we

must also affirm creativity and property. We cannot do away with one injustice by substituting another injustice. In the context of Scripture it is possible to affirm both justice and community, both property rights and generosity.

Second, we must be against inhuman productivity. We must stand against the concept of unlimited efficiency that has come out of the industrial West. The West has come to practice the notion that it does not matter if a process of production destroys man as long as it is efficient.

The Swiss have something to offer us. In Switzerland the working man has a long lunch break—an hour and a half—and he has time to go home, have lunch with his children who are home from school at the same time, drink a good cup of coffee, read a bit of the newspaper and even have time for a little nap before he goes back to work. This is inefficient, but it is much healthier than a half-hour snack break. What do we treasure? Humanness or productivity?

Or take another illustration, this time from the southern part of Germany in the area of Ravensburg and Tübingen. Here there are hundreds of small companies based on the Reformation consensus that it is more important that a master work with his apprentices than that he turn out a lot of products. More personally, I know one man who has deliberately kept his business small so he himself could be more human and could have more time for the Lord and the Lord's people.

I challenge you who are reading this book to step out and try something like this—to see the blessings of the Lord. He wants us to show something of the beauty and the wonder of a redeemed humanity.

Third, our understanding of property and humanity must lead us to insist on a Christian character to our homes. They should have a "community" atmosphere.

57

Even here we must insist on property so that there is something to share within the family. Without the property of a "home," a Christian would have little to share.

It doesn't have to be much. I remember one young man who came to L'Abri not long ago and remarked, "It's amazing that your bathrooms are clean." In all of the communities where he had been—and he had seen many—there were no clean bathrooms, nothing to share, no atmosphere, no character. And he was amazed at the difference, and then recognized the need to work creatively to produce that which can then be shared.

Fourth, we must respect human creativity despite the modern disregard for things themselves. We must look at things that men have made, contemplate them and enjoy them, because, if made well, they are works of art, works of human creativity. This means that we do not throw things away just to get an empty attic or an empty basement or an empty room somewhere. We ought not throw things away for the sake of throwing them away. As long as they show something of the creativity of the human being involved, we are throwing away part of the humanness of the maker, denying the validity of his creative activity.

This may make life a bit more complicated, because nobody wants a crowded attic, but it also makes life more real. We then stand in the continuity of men who show their humanity by the things they make. We stand in the continuity of the humanness of man as created in God's image in a world that is becoming increasingly more inhuman. And we find over and over that the contemplation of man's creativity will make more real our worship of the Creator of the man who has created the things that are before us.

God's creation speaks for God. Just look at it. Human creation speaks for man. Just look at it.

But if we become hyper-efficient, we will not love man,

we will have no compassion for him and for his creativity. The created object speaks of men the way the created world speaks of God.

And understand this: Usefulness must not decide whether a thing is beautiful or not. The creative activity that is expressed in a thing—that is what matters. It is there and it is beautiful and the contemplation of it must bring us to the Creator and really cause us to worship. Even the little flower that is too high for any eye to see is not wasted. God sees and enjoys it.

A little while ago some friends of ours moved into a chalet. And they kept above the back door the little sign reading, "Julius Hoffman," for he was the man who built it. He was a Christian and the house was built to be used by the Lord as a house for the Lord's people and as a base for his own preaching ministry. So they left the sign on it because it reminded them of the humanness of its builder.

For the same reason our family loves our own chalet, Gentiana, with all its nooks and crannies, all of the effort that it took to build it. I can hardly understand the prospective buyers whose only interest in buying it was to tear it down and put up a modern apartment chalet.

Humanness—that's what we must stress, if we are really the children of God, redeemed as men. Without it community dies. So I would encourage all of us to outdo each other in order to create, in order to have something to share. Let us not take offense at what others have. Let us be stimulated to create things of value ourselves. And let us cultivate spiritual values which we can also share, outdoing each other in godliness, in true faith, in true humanity and in true communion. Then indeed we will be able to speak the gospel in a living way.

The Circumference of Reality

"My perception stands in a system of coordinates that are set by the external world, the Bible, the continuity of time and the scope of all men across the world and throughout history. All of these are controls on each other, so that together they provide me with a view of reality that is more accurate than any one of them or than my perception of any one alone."

3

The eighteenth century, leading up to the outbreak of the French Revolution in 1789, was a time of tremendous change in the realm of traditional ideas. This change was not limited to political and social realities. Rather, the very concept of what is real was affected. The change, in fact, amounted to a reversal of the spiritual tradition of Europe since the Reformation, and it has subsequently led to what Eric Heller has called "an insidious deficiency in the concept of what is real."[1]

The Biblical Basis for the Knowledge of Reality

What concept of reality was displaced in this era of intellectual history? Essentially it was the notion that reality is a state of being that is independent of and does not derive itself from anything. It is effective existence and thus not dependent on our imagination or ideas. It is perceived in the act of cognition as an "opposite" outside of (or *even against*) my consciousness. Reality is also experienced in emotional-receptive and emotional-prospective acts. The former term describes reality acting upon me, as I am exposed to external limitations. The latter term describes anticipated events which exert a limitation on my actions in the expectation of a real situation to come.

This concept of reality was ultimately based on the idea that the Bible is God's propositional revelation. The image of God in man (Gen. 1:26) was understood to refer (among other things) to the essential relationship between God and man, whereby a continuity of categories existed from the character of the infinite-personal God to the finite-personal man. Attributes of God, revealed in Scripture, are then not only true to man, but also true to God and true to the impersonal creation.[2] They do not have an existence limited to man's perception but describe the actual form of what is there.

The Reformers in their return to the Bible as the Word of God pointed to a sufficient answer and a livable framework to heal the medieval grace-nature division that had resulted from man's view of himself as either too high (autonomous from God and revelation) or too low (the language used to refer to God was seen as essentially different from that describing man and at base unusable for living within the full circumference of life).

Genesis 1:26 and its context gave the framework for understanding that all of life was to be lived and enjoyed before a knowable God who had revealed himself so that man would have outside information that was not dependent upon his subjective consciousness.

The emphasis on the diversity of the members of the Godhead set the final backdrop as being personal. Real communication did exist between members of the Trinity forever (Jn. 17:24). God did not have to create in order to become personal in communication. And man, being personal, is not a misfit in an otherwise impersonal universe.

Consequently, we are not confined to the absurdity created by the acknowledgment that man's value necessarily depends on being able to ask questions in a universe where no absolute answer can be given. Rather, as men we can ask questions and look forward to answers which we can truly understand. Even after the Fall, we can realize that on the level of personality there is someone who can hear and respond to our complaints. Man does not have to be only a scream in a silent universe. Personality is not only real to us; we can also know that the personal God of the Bible has always existed. There is content to the *imago dei* in man.

Furthermore, the framework set in Genesis 1—3 gave the basis for the direct relationship of both man's prayers to God and God's revelation to man. God's knowledge of reality and man's knowledge of reality could have much in common, since man himself bore the *imago dei*. The finite bore a distinct resemblance to the infinite (Eph. 4:24; Col. 3:10; 2 Pet. 1:4). So, there was room not only for love and obedience, but also for knowledge about God, about man and about God's creation. In other words, the Bible explained the basis not only for man's understanding of the existence and character of God, but also for his understanding of God's creation, including personal man. It explained how man could understand that there was an objective existence independent of man's perception of it.

God the Creator has made an objective reality, which he, being infinite, knows objectively. This he communicates to man who, being finite, would otherwise have no way to be certain of perceiving anything outside of himself and his subjective consciousness.

The Incarnation of Christ is the most complete demonstration of this understanding. Christ, the second person of the Trinity, is the Logos, both the *ratio* and *oratio*, both the *mind* of God in his objective understanding of all reality and the *communication* of this truth (Jn. 1:1-18). He is objectivity which has become subjectively tangible (1 Jn. 1:1-4). The continuity of categories between the infinite-personal God of the Bible and the finite-personal

63

man made in the image of God undergirds the wonder of the Incarnation. Christ, the second person of the Trinity, continuing to be God (Phil. 2:6-8), took upon himself the attributes of man, who had been fashioned after his own image, his own attributes. This is the epistemological basis for the reasoning of Christ in his discussion with the Pharisees in John 10:30-36. The framework that allows men to be recipients of the Word of God for judgment in objective history not only permits but demands the possibility that God can become man without becoming someone essentially different.

What the Bible gave the Reformers, then, was not only the knowledge of God in such a way that individuals could return to fellowship with God through the work of Christ in his propitiatory death on the cross, but also a framework that established a view of reality larger than, but not contrary to, the individual's consciousness.

God has made an objective universe and personal beings who can perceive this universe truly. The Bible allows the individual not only to live with his perceptions but to measure these with the Word of God and the reality in which all individuals have to live. This is the basis for a profound enjoyment of reality. The dilemma of the objective-subjective relationship can thus be resolved for the Christian.

The more I live, therefore, in a full circle of life over a long period of time and the more I observe other people's circles of life, the more I can see the truth of the Bible's propositions (because I can verify them in a larger area). The more I can see the truth, the more justification I have to really live. Furthermore, both reality and the Bible impose a limitation on my own subjective imagination and consciousness-perception. Therefore, because I truly know what reality is I have a good chance of living in it and not being hurt by it.

The Bible gives man a sufficient framework within

which one finds interlocking, mutually supporting evidences and propositions. But the system is not circular. It does not prevent the possibility of error on my part, but rather allows me, if I am duty-bound by my findings, to live closer to what is there. I can now believe, in regard to all reality, that which is most reasonable, even if as a finite creature I will never understand all reality exhaustively.

What is real, then, is freed from the darkness of my individual perception. It exerts a control on my findings, which, rather than limiting me, allows me to really live, because there is reasonable certainty that what I perceive is actually there. I can live with my perception. My perception stands in a system of coordinates that are set by the external world, the Bible, the continuity of time and the scope of all men across the world and throughout history. All of these are controls on each other, so that together they provide me with a view of reality that is more accurate than any one of them or than my perception of any one alone.

The concept of reality coming out of the biblical thinking of the Reformation encompassed all of life in history. This is obvious in the life style of the people who, in the midst of liberation from the authoritarian rule of the Roman Catholic Church, found in historic Christianity a framework of belief in which the pursuit of science was proper, useful and in no way irreligious.[3] It was a time when all reality was taken to be the object of Christian interest.

Though it is not possible here, a detailed study of the cultural and sociological phenomena of seventeenth-century Holland would show this well.[4] There in a climate of political freedom and biblical philosophy the study of man's environment was made (all things were there to be weighed, measured, portrayed; above all, the study of man was not compartmentalized; there were no divisions between religion and life).

The rediscovery of the Bible, the openness to verification and the individual's willingness to bow before the God of the Bible for salvation and peace with God, were the reasons for the development of a truly human society. It was never perfect and often selfish. But historic Christianity gave the right epistemological climate for human existence. Work, sobriety, thrift and an emphasis on the value of labor and the common man were seen as essential.

In the relatively small communities, in which one was forcibly confronted by a diversity of situations and could not run from the hard things of life, where no escape routes existed, the necessarily close interdependence of technology, economics, art and philosophy brought about a more profound and circumferential understanding of man and his needs. This allowed a greater possibility to check on the claims of the Bible as well. Thus the area within the circle of reality was by necessity enlarged; one's subjective perceptions were more accurately controlled, because they had to correspond to a common reality.

The New Concept of Reality

The situation today is quite different. Reality is no longer seen as effective existence, no longer seen as a given. Rather, man desires autonomy. He wants to be free from all restriction in order to escape the moral controls of the personal God of Scripture as well as the mechanical controls of a technological age in which he as man no longer finds reason to assume his own humanness. In so establishing his autonomy, man finds himself at the end of a cave with his perception of things as the only light. Reality has thus become highly subjective. The continuity of categories (the perceiver and the thing perceived) in time (truth is not just the experience, but must stand in the continuum of time) and space (it must be true for all man in like situations) has been lost.

This change has been profoundly influenced by the thinkers of our age. Julien Benda points out that the intellectual was once a man who was known for his pursuit of an objective truth.[5] Therefore he was controlled in his findings by the need to check them against all reality over a period of time. One's propositions were open to judgment not just by others but by history itself and by the extent to which the man was able to live with his own propositions in the largest circle of life, in all areas of human existence. Heller describes this older mode of understanding as he explains how the traditional artist described a common vision in a surpassing fashion.[6] The requirement to correspond to that which was common constituted a form for artistic freedom.

Now, when all such controls are eliminated and any submission is seen as taking away the element of individual personality, we find disquieting results. A world in which truth and perception are set apart from "real" existence becomes strangely inhuman and deeply troublesome. Truth becomes equated with experience, modern contentless meditation and faith (as a leap into the dark), and then it is "perhaps nothing but an optical delusion enforced upon the eye by the dark prospect of a historical period and caused by a pathological narrowing in the common vision, by an insidious deficiency in the concept of what is real."[7]

We can groan with Heller when he writes, "And what a perverted doctrine of the human person had to be accepted by the world before the artists [or wider: any thinking person] could feel that he ceased to be a person precisely at the point where the real person should begin: in the act of submitting to an objective vision!"[8] He asks, then, "Where exactly grows the straw with which the bricks are made for the aesthetic edifice," or the edifice of meditation and pure experience?

The difficulty starts at the very point at which man's greatness finds its roots. For the Dutchmen of the early seventeenth century it was in the realization of the value of vision and observation; for a child it is the point of creating a life of fantasy and imagination (even exact fantasy, of a complete world with its own logical and consistent categories); and for any man it is the point at which man in his finiteness makes observations and statements of truth to which he attributes absolute truth value. In each case the difficulties start exactly at the point at which finite man frees himself from the need to control his observation by its correspondence to the external world. Each man must continue to live within the boundaries of the external world in spite of his own interpretation of that world and its boundaries.

The danger for each man rests not in his being able to perceive subjectively what is there independent of his perception. Nor is imagination to be despised but encouraged. Yet, when a man makes his perception or his imagination the only truth there is, he is inviting trouble. It is the loss of this limitation, the loss of the concept of objective truth, that is at the root of modern man's loss of reality. It was brought about and is characterized by a swing from the concept of the *necessity of reason* to the concept of the *sufficiency of reason.*[9]

The *necessity of reason* implies that reason is *necessary* to judge the credibility of any proposition. It affirms the capability of the human mind to proceed rationally in the continuity of categories, to judge a proposition by the way it corresponds to the world in which the proposer has to live independent of his proposition; it is simply the capability of the human mind to establish relationships of correspondence between individual experiences or propositions much in the same way a child strives and struggles to classify its environment in continuous categories and will from experiences in the past evaluate the present and anticipate the future. The *necessity of reason* relates to that phenomenon of the human mind that constantly strives, independent of the will, to establish a grid of propositions that mutually support each other. It is the basis of such notions as truth, right and wrong, antithesis, and the very nature of language itself, in that it refers to an objectively existing reality that can be perceived and then accurately described in language because that reality does not play tricks but is continuous.

By contrast, the *sufficiency of reason* deals with the change in the epistemological basis; it sees individual consciousness as the only source of truth. It frees the proposition from the need to correspond to any outside control. That is, a proposition can be true without referring to any objective reality. The result of this attitude is that the existence of any objective truth, including the real existence of an outside world, has become inconceivable or at least uncertain.

In the limits of this chapter, the epistemological change refers to the development of an emphasis on the autonomy of an individual's perception of reality. Autonomy is the desire to be a law unto oneself. Here it refers to the freedom from the requirement to correspond to the external world, within which all men have to live whether or not they perceive it or make propositions about it.

One is reminded of a Buddhist dilemma. The reality of the world cannot be changed by ascribing all categories and emotions only to the mind. Doing that does not change the reality of a child and an old man, youth and age, life and death, joy and sorrow. A child must be nursed in the middle of the night and an old man must eventually be buried.

There is an objective world that exists independently of our perception, and we cannot change it by merely reinterpreting it along the lines of our perception in the absence of any real categories. At the same time whether our perception and our categories are true does not depend on the intensity of our feeling, but rather on whether all men throughout history (space and time) are required to live with it continuously.

When I suggested above that the problem starts at the very point where man's greatness finds its roots, I was referring to the marvel that man is able to categorize his world and to perceive it and himself in it. But he must always allow some outside control for his perception, lest truth become only the one experience he has at any one time, without anything outside of the experience confirming its truth. For if man is the author of truth and the center of reality, then the immediate experience alone is anointed as the last reference point to all knowledge. That experience, however, can never by itself give the whole picture of what life and truth are all about.

If experience were its own interpreter, life would be like a film, already started when we enter the cinema and not finished before we are forced to leave. The meaning of the film would be only what we experienced when we were in the theater. The total framework would be missing and the whole film incomprehensible. What we need is the beginning and the end to give the continuity necessary to establish a grid of propositions. If, however, we have some knowledge of the beginning and the end, we have a way to establish a certainty that the propositions in question are true and not just subjective opinions.

Sources of the New Concept of Reality

We can arrive at a deficient position in regard to reality in two ways. One is to narrow down the circle of life to specialized areas, so that the circle against which we measure our propositions becomes ever and ever smaller. We see less and less of the depth and breadth of reality against which we can check the Bible and our own propositions about what is real. In other words, in my relationship to the Lord as well as to the realm of objective reality, I lack the very thing that the Bible allows me, that is, an outside control, so that my perception is not phantastic, but true to what is there (the form I have to live with).

Our own age fosters the narrowing of the circle of what is real by pushing us into extreme specialization. We think that we know something, even though it's only in a very small sector of reality. But we can't really be sure because too few others have worked in the same area. We are thus kings without subjects. Nonetheless, we are able to live quite well with this uncertainty because there is no need in an affluent society to learn to cope with a diversity of situations. We can always defer to another specialist, rather than expose ourselves to a tough situation and be forced to handle it creatively.

The second way that we arrive at a deficient concept of reality is the one that rationalistic man succumbed to as soon as he freed himself by an act of the will from dependence on an outside control. We find this in the development of thought from the time of the Enlightenment. The Bible gives me a *right* to catalog, understand and investigate God's creation, because I am placed as vice-regent of God into the midst of his creation. Reality has been made by the infinite-personal God who has spoken to tell me that what I perceive and what I live with in the full circumference of life is really there. There is, therefore, a correspondence between my perception and reality.

But note the immediate danger. We may simply take that *right* from Scripture and then forget its source. Actually I am obliged to submit my perception to the one granting that right. In the absence of such openness to control, my perception remains the only truth. It becomes freed from the need to correspond to and be checked by an objective reality. It opens the way for me to propose non-sense and even insanity as truth, for the propositions are freed from what in the past always allowed for some civility: that propositions were not taken seriously unless they spoke of the real world that all men live in.

This change follows consistently from the epistemology of the Enlightenment. The strength of the culture of seventeenth-century Holland rested in the rediscovery of the Bible and through it in the reaffirmation of the value of man, both for dignity and for destruction. Man's finiteness and the limitations of man's perceptions were acknowledged. Only in being subject to outside information could truth ever exist in any meaningful way for man. Now man is left with only his momentary experience, and then with only the experience of an experience, he has to attach to such apparitions not only truth value, but also meaning and direction for all of life.

Descartes' attempt to free himself from all preconceived notions and to doubt everything in order to arrive at something more true is noble. But in the end he succeeds only in deifying man. For to reconstruct from the base on up all systems and all knowledge sets up the human perception as the sole criterion for truth; truth is subject only to the individual's reason. Reality independent of the individual's perception soon not only becomes inadmissable evidence, but is as evidence inconceivable. It is a situation accurately described in Romans 1 when Paul says that men became "futile in their thinking and their senseless minds were darkened. Claiming to be wise, they became fools" (vv. 21-22). For there is no guarantee that the creations of the human mind, no matter how noble their beginning, are necessarily true.

In his *Discourse on Method*, Descartes says:

I wished to give myself entirely to the search after

Truth. I thought that it was necessary for me to . . .
reject as absolutely false everything as to which I could
imagine the least ground of doubt, in order to see if
afterwards there remained anything in my belief that
was entirely certain. Thus, because our senses sometimes deceive us, I wished to suppose that nothing is
just as they cause us to imagine it to be. . . . I resolved
to assume that everything that ever entered my mind
was no more true than the illusion of my dreams. But
immediately afterwards I noticed that whilst I thus
wished to think all things false, it was absolutely essential that the "I" who thought this should be some-
what.[10]

"Cogito ergo sum" (I think, therefore, I am) became the
"first principle" of his philosophy.

He continues to say that he might assume "as a general
rule, that the things which we conceive very clearly and
distinctly are all true—remembering, however, that
there is some difficulty in ascertaining which are those
which we distinctly conceive."[11]

But he recognizes the problem of accepting oneself as
the only authority when he continues, in the *First Meditation*, to point out the limitation of anything that has the
human perception as the only reference point without
the possibility of establishing an integrated set of propositions about truth:

All that up to the present time I have accepted as most
true and certain I have learned either from the senses
or through the senses; but it is sometimes proved to
me that these senses are deceptive, and it is wiser
sometimes not to trust entirely to any thing by which
we have once been deceived.[12]

In the luxury afforded to Descartes by being early in
the development of the rationalistic epistemology, he
decides to trust the senses in the perception of things
about which "we cannot reasonably have any doubt."[13]

73

But such an appeal to *reasonableness* outside of a structure that in itself gives validity to reason will be no help, as the subsequent history of thought as well as the present generation's horrible experiment in actual living show. To say that all those whose perception differs with his are "mad" is only to make his particular, uncheckable reasonableness absolute, which in turn may be only a kinder expression for a similar madness.

For the problem remains the same.

How often has it happened to me that in the night I dreamt that I found myself on this particular place, ... whilst in reality I was lying ... in bed! At this moment it does indeed seem to me that it is with eyes awake that I am looking at this paper. . . . But in thinking over this I remind myself that on many occasions I have in sleep been deceived by similar illusions, and in dwelling carefully on this reflection I see so manifestly that there are no certain indications by which we may clearly distinguish wakefulness from sleep that I am lost in astonishment. And my astonishment is such that it is almost capable of persuading me that I now dream.[14]

Here we find the beginning of the problem that has shaped the thought of Western culture to our own day.

In the philosophical system of Immanuel Kant the problem appears again and a shift occurs. According to Kant, knowledge can be gained by sense perception (theoretical knowledge from *theoria,* or view), by pure reason independent of sense perception and by practical reason which begins from a consideration of man's moral nature.

None of these ways to knowledge, however, allows man to burst the limitations of subjectivity and to know truly, if not exhaustively, objective existence. The reason for this is that all knowledge that originates in the human mind (or makes impressions upon it) is subject to the finite categories of man's perception. One can never arrive at the knowledge of a thing-in-itself (*Ding-an-sich*), nor can he be told by a God who could know the thing-in-itself, for God, being infinite, cannot speak directly and understandably to finite man. Even *time* and *space*, according to Kant, are subjective categories; they are imposed on man's sense perceptions by man's mind; they are not qualities of objective reality.

Kant did, however, wish to establish that an infinite God exists. But because Kant saw personality as a limitation to infinity, he was left with a God who could not have a character and could not speak personally and directly to man concerning the nature of the external universe. In the area of *theoretical knowledge,* man can only perceive data (there can be no certainty about the thing perceived). In the area of *pure reason* man can have an idea about real existence without any content of data. In the area of *practical reason* man has an unverifiable assumption that immortality, the soul, God, must exist in order to give validity to the moral nature of man. But we must understand that, if all man's knowledge is true only to man and not to itself and if man's senses can deceive him in regard to ordinary reality, they can also deceive him in regard to God.

Descartes' appeal to a good God is therefore not essentially different from an unjustified projection of man's high view of personality onto God. With Kant, therefore, the existence of a God with a definite character was excluded, and with that fell the last hope that there is anything more to our sense perceptions than human creativity or wishful thinking.

Kant's views were dressed in religious language that is deceptive because of its expression of piety. But when God becomes the wholly other (the *totaliter aliter* of Kant), then nothing can be said about him that would have any reference to finite categories, that is, categories that men can understand, then even his existence is called into question. And consequently human existence, no longer having an infinite reference point, is itself no longer reasonable or sure.

In the realm of morals, Sedlmayr has pointed out that as rationalistic man has piously removed the anthropomorphic from God (that is, freed him from human categories), he has also removed the theomorphic from man (that is, freed him from objective categories).[15] In other words, when God ceased being man-like, man ceased being God-like. Man is then left with no way out of the chain that he dreams that he dreams....

Kierkegaard, or at least his influence on Western thought, took the problem further. If there was to be any communication between the timeless-spaceless God of Kant and man in his space-time limitations, it had to be indirect: Its nature was *totaliter aliter*. One could no longer approach God with questions about content and truth. With Kierkegaard one enters the realm of unverifiable myth. Mesas has said, "Here starts the drama: under the disguise of an humble acknowledgement of our phenomenological hindrances, we complain bitterly for living in a complete absence of justification."[16] It is today's supreme irony that rationalistic man denies the knowability of God and finds himself subsequently in the position of having to acknowledge "the necessity of an infinite absolute Entity [Being] by the declaration of the worthlessness of man's aspirations and perceptions in a world that has no such Entity."[17] This is very much related to Kierkegaard's concept of Christianity without certainty, which may be understandable in terms of his own struggle in the Danish church in the nineteenth century, but influenced much modern thought through its affirmation of a split-level view of truth.

Wittgenstein, for example, was profoundly touched by Kierkegaard and took his thought another step. Since

on the basis of rationalistic thought the only existing
reality is the one I can talk about, and language (the "defining mystery of man"[18]) is the creation of man, there
will never again be any certainty that language describes
a reality that is already there. The relationship of language to reality as paralleling that of shadow to sub-
stance cannot be accepted. What can give us any assur-
ance that, as Steiner says in reference to Wittgenstein's
Tractatus, "a fact may well be a veil spun by language to
shroud the mind from reality"?[19] Can reality be spoken
of when speech is merely a kind of infinite regression
of words being spoken of other words?

In this kind of system one can have no confidence
that there is an objective reality that offers itself to man to
be touched, cataloged, described. Reality is reduced to
the immediate experience, to the untouchable "more
real" of meditation. By its very nature reality need not
correspond to the circle of life all men must live in. Real
reality, or, as Hesse says, the secret of the League,[20] cannot be known in the categories of reason and truth. Reality withdraws therefore, for the modern man, into the
realm of the mysterious, or at least the private. The circle
of reality in practice and the concept of reality in thought
are by and large insidiously deficient.

Such a narrow view and experience of a reality that is
reduced finally to subjective opinion is freed from the
judgment of more general categories and from history.
And with it disappears any conceivable and irrefutable
witness to man's reality!

This would be sad enough if it remained only in the
realm of thought and theoretical discussion. But the life
style of our generation is a demonstration in practice
of this pattern of modern thought. Some children of the
surrounding mentality stand in a dark cave surrounded
only by their own light; others carefully choose indepen-
dence from the circle of reality as an excuse for their

selfishness.

It is here where biblical Christianity gives both framework and dimension for the practice of an alternative. Here we find a communication by and about God that relates to all creation and can be checked within it. Here man can have greater certainty as he stands in the midst of life in a full circle of living situations. Work, creativity, property within the limitations of community, a relationship of concern for society—all these seen in the order of the Bible after the fall of man not only will help prevent the chaos and heightened insanity of people living only for their own experiences, but also will be found to correspond to the circumference of life within which man can live and be real.

The
Limits of
Selfishness

"It is only by taking up our cross and denying ourselves that we can be fulfilled as creatures in the reality of God's creation."

4

We have seen already one of the dilemmas of rationalism, that philosophic stance which focuses on man himself as the one who determines the truth of what is and
which, if taken to its logical conclusion, results in the notion that truth equals subjective opinion. For if man
alone from inside himself determines the truth of what
is, he is left with only a subjective conviction. We could
discuss how this subjectivism means that ultimately every
man is out for himself, and that even within each individual man selfish, hedonistic desires are pitted against
each other. Such rationalism is at the root of the breakdown of both civic order and psychic order. The alienation from God leads to both an alienation from external
reality and an alienation within internal reality.

"Trapped inside his private universe, each man lives
his private life," someone has said. We often live with a
merely subjective faith rather than with a faith based on
the reality of God's existence. We place our emphasis on
feeling rather than on intellectual content. And that is
how we get into trouble. For when the feeling goes, our
world collapses.

In the area of philosophy, we have traced this result to

a deficiency in the concept of what is real. But the same deficiency is often seen in our own attitude to living as Christians in God's world. So often our own reality becomes too heavily subjective. And this subjective emphasis leads us to look only at ourselves and thus fail to see our relationship to the rest of God's reality.

History, including the history of our own lives, becomes unreal to us. We see only the present. We forget that we don't need everything at once. For we will probably still be alive, most of us, in twenty years.

Men around us become unreal as well, because the only man who exists for each man is himself, and so we have little compassion for each other. We act as though our problems were far greater than anybody else's. We think that we are the ones who are always at the bottom of the ladder. Self-centeredness—that's the heart of our problem.

The Bible, on the contrary, stresses the reality not just of ourselves but of others, of the world and of God, and answers all of our problems in the context of the whole. God insists on a radical redirection of our self-centered outlook so that it fits into total reality. Here truth is seen as truth, and reality is seen as the complexity of God's creation and God's redeeming action in history. Suddenly things begin to fit together, and reality is no longer made up of just our subjective opinion, our subjective mannishness, our subjective sorrow.

When we redirect our perspective, we will see that things do not have to fit together in "me as an individual" but rather that they fit together in the fact that God is there and that he is an infinite-personal God and so not one of our individualities is lost. We will discover that we are all related to God the Creator who has made us all individually and in whom all things are fitly framed together. This is the only way we can get away from our own finite conception of reality, our finite conception of

evil and of pain that we like to feel and dwell on in ourselves.

Such a perspective is indeed the answer to Jean Paul
Sartre's statement that all finite things need an infinite
reference point. Sartre never had such a reference point.
The claim that Christianity is true is based on the fact
that all reality comes from God and that we as individuals
are only part of the reality. We do not create the reality
from ourselves. And yet the idea that God is the infinite-
personal God and has made a reality which is personal
alters deeply our own attitude both to God and to the
reality he has made. It is the purpose of this chapter to
concentrate on our attitude toward reality especially in
the area of material things.

Rich Man/Poor Man

The Bible teaches that we must not attach ourselves to
material things, to riches of any kind, because they are
not a sufficient integration point. We are to deny any
attachment to riches as such. Jesus told his disciples,
"Truly, I say to you, it will be hard for a rich man to enter
the kingdom of heaven" (Mt. 19:23). The message of
the Old Testament is just as insistent: "If riches increase,
set not your heart on them" (Ps. 62:10) and "Riches do
not last for ever" (Prov. 27:24). It is indeed folly to set our
heart on riches, for if we set our heart on something that
passes away, then we too will equally pass away. All our
energy, all our life, dwindles away.

Moreover, if we set our heart on something that we
have created, we have set our heart on something less
than we are because it depends on us. And so, rather
than acknowledging that God is the one who has made
us, we have taken as our god something we have made.

In Proverbs we read: "One man pretends to be rich,
yet has nothing; another pretends to be poor, yet has
great wealth. The ransom of a man's life is his wealth, but

a poor man has no means of redemption" (Prov. 13:7-8). As we noted above, the rich man is valued not because he is a person but because he is rich, and the richer he is the more dangerous and worrisome life is because all of his energies are centered upon the maintenance of his riches. The poor man, on the other hand, is esteemed as a man.

In the Sermon on the Mount, Jesus further comments on the place of riches in human life: "Do not lay up for yourselves treasures on earth, where moth and rust consume and where thieves break in and steal, but lay up for yourselves treasure in heaven, where neither moth nor rust consumes and where thieves do not break in and steal. For where your treasure is, there will your heart be also" (Mt. 6:19-21). Later in the sermon he says that men should not be anxious about the material aspects of life, what they should eat or drink or wear, for "your heavenly Father knows that you need them all. But seek first his kingdom and his righteousness, and all these things shall be yours as well" (Mt. 6:32-33). In the parable of the sower he points out that the "cares of the world and the delight in riches" choke the Word of God so that it becomes unfruitful.

References such as these could be multiplied, but they serve to show the essence of the teaching of both the Old and the New Testament: Men are not to attach themselves to riches, for in the end their very lives become forfeit.

Some Christians see this and find it very easy not to attach themselves to riches. Young people rarely have any riches anyway, and so many of them think it is nice that they do not have to attach themselves to riches. They tend to be proud of the fact that they are relatively poor. But let us be careful. If we attach ourselves to *anything* that is less than God, it will corrupt. Anything less than God will pass away, and the one who has attached himself to it will have nothing left.

But there is a positive side as well as a negative. We are not to depend on riches; we are to depend on God. The Pharisees tried to trip up Jesus at just this point. They asked, "Is it lawful to pay taxes to Caesar, or not?" (Mt. 22:17). But Jesus knew what was at stake. Aware of their antagonism, he said, "Why put me to the test, you hypocrites? Show me the money for the tax" (v. 18). When they had given him a coin and acknowledged that it had Caesar's inscription on it, Jesus said, "Render therefore to Caesar the things that are Caesar's, and to God the things that are God's" (v. 21).

At first it seems that Jesus is saying that there is a part of life that belongs to Caesar and another part that belongs to God. But that is not his point. What he is saying is that if you have a coin with Caesar's standard on it, it belongs to Caesar. Give it to Caesar. But all reality belongs to God, both Caesar's coin and even Caesar himself, not just what is left over after you have given the penny to Caesar.

The Christian and the Cross

Just as we are not to depend on something that is outside of ourselves which is less than God, we are not to depend on ourselves as such. All reality—including us—must be seen in relationship to the infinite-personal God. Jesus teaches us throughout the New Testament that we must take up our cross daily and follow him.

In Jesus' instruction to the twelve disciples just before sending them out to minister on their own, he says, "He who loves father or mother more than me is not worthy of me; and he who loves son or daughter more than me is not worthy of me; and he who does not take his cross and follow me is not worthy of me. He who finds his life will lose it, and he who loses his life for my sake will find it" (Mt. 10:37-40). In Luke 14:27-29 we find an additional emphasis: "Whoever does not bear his own cross and come after me, cannot be my disciple. For which of you, desiring to build a tower, does not first sit down and count the cost, whether he has enough to complete it? Otherwise, when he has laid a foundation, and is not able to finish, all who see it begin to mock him." Imagine the uncompleted tower. Just the foundation and walls are there, no roof, and as the weather beats upon it, the tower just disintegrates.

Jesus continues, "Or what king, going to encounter another king in war, will not sit down first and take counsel whether he is able with ten thousand to meet him who comes against him with twenty thousand? And if not, while the other is yet a great way off, he sends an embassy and asks terms of peace. So therefore, whoever of you does not renounce all that he has cannot be my disciple" (Lk. 14:31-33).

So Christ says two things: If you are to follow me, you must take up your cross daily, and you must count the cost. Discipleship involves all of life. It involves a turning away from our selfishness, a recentering on the Lordship of Christ and on the reality of God's existence.

Jesus' teaching about the cross contains a second point: It is only by taking up our cross and denying ourselves that we can be fulfilled as creatures in the reality of God's creation. Consider the passage in Matthew 16 where Jesus announces that he is going up to Jerusalem to be crucified, claiming in fact that that is why he has come into the world. Peter is disturbed and begins to rebuke Jesus: "God forbid, Lord! This shall never happen to you" (Mt. 16:22). But Jesus turns to him and uses the strongest words: "Get behind me, Satan! You are a hindrance to me; for you are not on the side of God, but of men" (v. 23). In other words, "Why are you so selfish, Peter? Why do you not live in the reality where God is the beginning, the center and the end?"

Then he turns to his disciples and says, "If any man would come after me, let him deny himself and take up his cross and follow me. For whoever would save his life will lose it, and whoever loses his life for my sake will find it" (vv. 24-25). The same verse is repeated in Mark 8:34-35 and Luke 9:23-24. In John 12:25, it is expressed slightly differently: "He who loves his life loses it, and he who hates his life in this world will keep it for eternal life." It is interesting that Jesus does not say that we will have life in "life eternal" but that we will keep our present life unto life eternal. "Eternal life" begins now.

All this ties in with the rich young ruler of Matthew 19. He has tried to keep all the laws; in fact, he says he has kept all those that Christ mentions. But when Jesus says to him, "If you would be perfect, go, sell what you possess and give to the poor, and you will have treasure in heaven; and come, follow me," that is too much. The denial of self-centeredness, the willingness to take his place in reality and not to make himself the center of the only reality that exists is a hard, costly thing to do—too hard, too costly. But for those who would be disciples, it is the only way. Not only that: It is the only way in which we can really be fulfilled as human beings.

There is a third aspect to Jesus' teaching about the cross. To take up one's cross daily means a drastic redirection of every part of our life; it means putting God rather than ourselves at the center of everything that we do and not just at the center of our "spiritual" lives.

The statement that he who loses his life shall find it appears to be self-contradictory, even foolish. We read in 1 Corinthians, for example:

For the word of the cross is folly to those who are perishing, but to us who are being saved it is the power of God. For it is written, "I will destroy the wisdom of the wise, and the cleverness of the clever I will thwart."

Where is the wise man? Where is the scribe? Where

87

is the debater of this age? Has not God made foolish the wisdom of the world? (1 Cor. 1:18-20)

Paul does not mean that the gospel is foolishness either for the Christian or for the non-Christian who is interested in truth. It is indeed not folly that God would give salvation but rather that man should seek it himself. Yet to the man who is seeking salvation for himself and who has set himself up as the arbiter of what is true, the gospel appears to be folly. The gospel is folly only to those who set themselves up as the "wise of the earth."

The center of God's redeeming work in history is that Jesus Christ, the second person of the Trinity, became man, was obedient to God the Father and died on the cross for each man who casts himself on Christ and accepts redemption through him. It is of central significance that this same Jesus was raised from the dead and sits on the right hand of God from whence he will come again and we shall see him as he is. To be sure, this is not foolishness but wisdom itself.

We see the folly of modern philosophy and of modern moral programs in the breakdown of society and the subsequent suffering of man. The life style of our modern age with all its wealth is destroying individual man wherever it meets him. What is needed is not just "salvation through Christ" but a redirected and wholly changed life style lived under the reign of God. It involves a true fulfillment of all human aspiration.

What then is to happen to the man who takes up his cross daily? Jesus did not leave us in the dark, for when Peter said, "Lo, we have left everything and followed you. What then shall we have?" Jesus said,

Truly, I say to you, in the new world, when the Son of man shall sit on his glorious throne, you who have followed me will also sit on twelve thrones, judging the twelve tribes of Israel. And every one who has left houses or brothers or sisters or father or mother or

children or lands, for my name's sake, will receive a
hundredfold, and inherit eternal life. But many that
are first will be last, and the last first. (Mt. 19:27-30)
This passage is immediately followed by the parable of
the man who hired laborers for his vineyard, paying each
man the same wage regardless of when he was hired
during the day. And that parable ends with the same sentence: "So the last will be first, and the first last" (20:16).
So the end of chapter 19 and the beginning of chapter 20
form a unit.

But look at the tremendous humanness of Peter. Peter
believes that he and the disciples have given up all. So
Jesus says that he will then have his reward. He says,
"You have taken up your cross. There will be definite results, definite rewards." But Jesus is teaching Peter that
there is a real danger that the cross will become a means
of self-esteem, a means of self-centeredness again. How
easy it will be to say proudly, "Well, I am looking only to
God to give me the reward. I'm not tied to material
things." Jesus says, "You must not only not reach out for
riches but you must not be proud to have nothing." We
should be willing to be what God wants us to be, neither
proud in riches, nor proud in self, but proud in God.

What does it mean to be proud in God? What does it
mean to get out of our self-pity, to get out of the trap of
seeing ourselves in the worst possible position, thinking
everybody else is better off? What does it mean that whoever loses his life for Christ's sake shall find it? The Old
Testament gives us many examples of real people in real
situations.

Abraham
Abraham was called by God to come out of a culture
where he was esteemed. It was a culture of comfort, of
steam baths and social sophistication. God led him first to
Haran and then into the wilderness of Canaan. And it

was really a wilderness in every way—ecological and human. In worship and art, it was pagan and crude. But Abraham followed God because he knew that God knew what was good for him. He also knew that his citizenship was not in this present world. It was neither in Ur nor in Haran nor in Canaan nor in Egypt. As Paul later said, "Our commonwealth [our citizenship] is in heaven" (Phil. 3:20). We are sojourners on this earth and in the words of the writer of Hebrews, "We have no lasting city, but we seek the city which is to come" (Heb. 13:14).

So Abraham did not make his present situation the center of all reality, and he did not pity himself because he had been led into the wilderness. Nor should we. When God calls us into a "wilderness," we ought not to say, "God, I don't want it." Rather before God we should be willing to say, "God, you do it. I trust you, I am proud of you, proud of the kind of God you are."

Because Abraham did this, he became the father of the Jewish nation and the Christ came through it to all nations. Leaving his own background, he became the friend of God (Is. 41:8; Jas. 2:23). In other words, Abraham lost his life but found it. Abraham became last but was found to be first.

Moses

We could also take the case of Moses. He was raised in Pharaoh's court and thus came to know a sophisticated life (Acts 7:22). But when he saw himself as the deliverer of the Jewish workers, they turned against him (Acts 7:25). He had to leave Egypt because he had slain an Egyptian. His deed became well known and Pharaoh threatened to kill him. So Moses went out into the desert and immediately life became less complicated. There were the roaming pastures, the desert brush, sheep and cattle, and he had a wife and two sons, the comfort and the ease of life. Certainly this was not the intellectual center of Egypt, but here was an easier life and it was nice.

But Moses did not become proud of this life. True, God had to convince Moses that he was the man to do the job that God had in mind—leading the Israelite nation from Egypt to the promised land. Moses had no more confidence in himself and argued that he was not a speaker and the people were not going to listen to him. But he was willing to act on his confidence in the God who is there, the God who said, "I am who I am," and who identified himself as the God of Abraham, Isaac and Jacob (Ex 3:13-15), rooting his existence down into his faithfulness in verifiable history. By obeying God, Moses went back into a situation where he could not be sure of his life, and God used him to become a prophet of the law of God and the leader of the great Exodus. Moses lost the life he preferred and found real life before the living God.

David and Solomon

David too represents what happens when a man puts himself in a proper relationship to God and others. Even after he had been anointed by Samuel, and Saul was no longer king, David did not covet the title of king so long as Saul lived. After he had cut off the skirt of Saul's robe in the cave in the wilderness of Engedi, "David's heart smote him, because he had cut off Saul's skirt. He said to his men, 'The LORD forbid that I should do this thing to my lord, the LORD's anointed, to put forth my hand against him, seeing he is the LORD's anointed' " (1 Sam. 24:5-6). It was the willingness not to be self-centered or to take the course of history into his own hands that allowed David to become the man he was—the writer of many psalms and, indeed, a progenitor of a much greater, Jesus the Christ.

We have a further example in Solomon, David's more immediate son. We read in 2 Chronicles 1:7-12 how God

91

appeared to Solomon and asked him what he really wanted most. And Solomon said, "O LORD God, let thy promise to David my father be now fulfilled, for thou hast made me king over a people as many as the dust of the earth. Give me now wisdom and knowledge to go out and come in before this people, for who can rule this thy people, that is so great?" (vv. 9-10).

God's answer is instructive:

Because this was in your heart, and you have not asked possessions, wealth, honour, or the life of those who hate you, and have not even asked long life, but have asked wisdom and knowledge for yourself that you may rule my people over whom I have made you king, wisdom and knowledge are granted to you. I will also give you riches, possessions, and honour, such as none of the kings had who were before you, and none after you shall have the like. (vv. 11-12)

The lesson is clear. Because Solomon did not take pity upon himself nor ask God to make him wealthy or great but rather yielded to be what God wanted him to be, a wise ruler over God's people, God gave him wisdom and then added to it wealth and life. Solomon lost his life but found it.

Abraham, Moses, David and Solomon—all four refused to be selfish. They took up their cross, they did not receive an easy life—none of them—but they knew God and received God's reward. They received that which God granted them in the total reality of history in a fallen and therefore imperfect world, but they received in large measure a fulfilled life.

Elijah

The Bible also records accounts of men who did not always take the selfless way. One of the more interesting cases is Elijah, for Elijah had taken the selfless way and had been a servant of God for many years before he turned inward and became discouraged. 1 Kings 17—19 contains the whole story and it is instructive to read it at one sitting.

Elijah is serving God under the reign of King Ahab and the wicked Queen Jezebel. Ahab and Jezebel have led Israel into a completely idolatrous worship of Baal, and Elijah prophesies for God before Ahab that it will not rain for three-and-a-half years. And it doesn't. God then leads Elijah to the brook Cherith and commands the ravens to feed him. Then God leads him to the widow at Zarephath, and he stays with her for the rest of the three-and-a-half years, God miraculously supplying their need for food and a cure for the mortal illness of the widow's son.

God then sends Elijah back to Ahab to prophesy rain, and there follows the contest between Elijah and the priests of Baal. The question is, Who is real, Jehovah or Baal? The priests beat themselves all day long so that the fire will come down and take up the sacrifice, and nothing happens. Then Elijah lays out the wood, soaks it with water until water stands in the trenches all about it and the wood is thoroughly wet. Elijah asks the God of the Bible to show that he is God by bringing down fire onto the sacrifice. And the fire comes and takes the sacrifice and licks up the water.

After this, the priests of Baal are put to death (because they had deliberately turned the people from serving God), and Ahab begins to listen again to Elijah the prophet of the true God. When Elijah prophesies rain, Ahab believes him and the rain comes.

And yet, after all of this—after all the trial and tribulation of living in the desert, being fed by ravens and having God work mighty deeds—Elijah stumbles. For Jezebel sends a message to him saying, "So may the gods do to me, and more also, if I do not make your life as the life of one of them [the priests who had been slain] this time tomorrow" (1 Kings 19:2). And the chronicler writes that Elijah "arose and went for his life," fleeing into the wilderness.

Just think what Elijah had gone through. God had showed him the tremendous reality of his existence by taking up the sacrifice that was soaked with water against all chance, to make sure that it was God who was acting. Ahab had turned to listen to Elijah. And still, when Jezebel threatened, Elijah got discouraged. He became petulant. He felt sorry for himself, got scared and ran into the desert. Instead of seeing what God had in mind, he became self-centered. He looked at himself and felt sorry for a while, and God could not use him.

But God spoke to him in the wilderness and Elijah saw again that God was God and came again to be of some service to his Lord. What a testimony to the way in which a man loses his life and finds it or seeks his life and loses it! For when Elijah kept his eye on God and cared not for his own life, he found his life, but when he turned inward, feared for his safety and fled into the desert, he truly lost his life for a time. Even a man who has served God can lose the perspective which has made his life meaningful and for a time at least revert to selfishness.

Jonah

In Jonah we have a similar situation. Jonah is sent to Nineveh to preach to the people and to warn them that unless they repent they will all be destroyed. And Nineveh was a huge city for its time, having a population of well over 100,000 people and being as the text says "an exceedingly great city, three days' journey in breadth" (Jon. 3:3). Jonah enters the city a day's journey and proclaims this message: "Yet forty days, and Nineveh shall be overthrown!" (Jon. 3:4).

Then, we are told, Nineveh repents and God does not bring destruction upon the city. But this displeases

Jonah. He is angry. Why? Because he has become self-centered. He has been the prophet, he has walked a day's journey into the city and he has delivered the message that unless they repent destruction will come in forty days, and the message has been believed and acted upon.

But now Jonah feels that he is a prophet whose prophecy has not come true, for the city has not been destroyed. And he feels sorry for himself. Then God in a gentle but definite way says to him, "Jonah, are you not so sorry for yourself that you do not see how much I am sorry for the 100,000 people in the city of Nineveh? Jonah, why are you so selfish?" And God points this out to him that Jonah might live again in a reality where God is the center. Caring less for his own position, he became the man through whose preaching many repented and escaped certain destruction in their moment of history.

Abigail and Nabal

The story of Abigail and Nabal in 1 Samuel 25 focuses on the distinct difference between its two chief characters. On the one hand there is Nabal. He is a very rich man; he has 3,000 sheep and 3,000 goats and is living a good life in David's kingdom. But he is a churlish man, a grouch, self-centered, tough, a man who gives everybody a hard time. His wife, Abigail, points out that his very name characterizes him—*Nabal*, "obstinate fool." His folly is well displayed in the way he reacts to David's call for a portion of his harvest of wool. David had protected Nabal from raids by marauders and thus he owed David a certain share in the harvest. But he refuses to pay a thing.

The other character in the story is Abigail. She is a woman "of good understanding and beautiful" (v. 3), and her wisdom shines out through her actions in the chapter. She knows that David has helped Nabal and his flock, protecting them against thieves, and she knows that when David's request for his fair share of the shearing has been rejected, David will respond with force.

So Abigail goes to meet David who is indeed coming in strength, having said, "Surely in vain have I guarded all that this fellow has in the wilderness, so that nothing was missed of all that belonged to him; and he has returned me evil for good. God do so to David and more also, if by morning I leave so much as one male of all who belong to him" (vv. 21-22). Abigail says not a word to Nabal but puts together "two hundred loaves, and two skins of wine, and five sheep ready dressed, and five measures of parched grain, and a hundred clusters of raisins, and two hundred cakes of figs" (v. 18), and loads them upon asses and goes out to meet David and to atone for the insolence of her husband.

She goes down on her knees before David and says, "Forgive me, my husband is a fool." That is no easy thing to do. She could go over to David and leave Nabal all by himself, but that would be selfish. She could decide not to stick to her husband and feel sorry for herself. Instead she tries to keep God's law, and that means that she has to come out from her husband and tell David what a fool her husband is. But she does it in a very clever way.

She says to David, "David, look, if you revenge yourself on Nabal, you violate God's law because God says 'I am the avenger.'" That is, she protects Nabal and she keeps David from sinning at the same time. For David has been selfish too, and in this meeting, we find two people deciding not to be selfish, deciding rather to live in the total reality where God is the center, thereby not breaking God's law but receiving a blessing.

David says to Abigail,

Blessed be the LORD, the God of Israel, who sent you this day to meet me! Blessed be your discretion, and blessed be you, who have kept me this day from bloodguilt and from avenging myself with my own hand! For as surely as the LORD the God of Israel lives, who has restrained me from hurting you, unless you had made haste and come to meet me, truly by morning there had not been left to Nabal so much as one male. (vv. 32-34)

David recognizes his selfishness. He thanks Abigail for her help. Abigail gives David what was expected, namely food, and Abigail leaves. God takes care of the situation for both of them, because they both decide not to be selfish at that moment.

There is an interesting aftermath. When Abigail returns to her husband, she finds him feasting like a king and "very drunk" (v. 36). So she waits until the next morning and when Nabal is sober she tells him what she has done. "And his heart died within him, and he became as a stone. And about ten days later the LORD smote Nabal; and he died" (vv. 37-38). When David hears about this, he sends for Abigail and takes her to be his wife. She gets a most desirable person for a husband, and he a wife with a sensitive understanding of the complexities of real life.

If we try to carry out our own schemes with ourselves at the center, it will not do. Why do we not learn, individually, all of us, to have God at the center of all reality and the center of our life? Why do we not learn to be less selfish, to lose our life that we might gain life?

The Problem of Comparing

It was precisely this that Christ was trying to teach Peter in the parable of the vineyard. Each servant was hired into the vineyard at a different hour during the day but each received the same wage. To complain against this is precisely the same kind of selfishness that we have seen with Elijah and Jonah and Nabal. There is a danger for Peter. When Peter says, "Look, I've given up everything, what will be my reward?" Jesus replies, "You will have your reward. There is no one that gives up everything that does not have a reward. It will be a just reward and actually more than you deserve because I delight in rewarding you." But the danger comes at exactly that point in which Peter, just like all of us, would turn around and compare himself with other children of God.

We are called to be God's as he calls us. Our relationship is to be primarily to him and not to each other. Everyone in the parable gets what he agrees on when he starts to work. Those who work for twelve hours agree to a certain sum of money and receive it. Because it is the master's pleasure to give the same amount to the person who only works for one hour should be of no consequence to the man who works for twelve. It is not right to compare one to the other. To do so can lead to nothing but envy and failure to be fulfilled.

But the Bible emphasizes that God is fair to each one of us, individually. The trouble only starts when we compare ourselves to each other, whether this be in the area of reward, financial success, being married or not being married, or whatever. Furthermore, when we set up a standard to measure our spirituality, say, by counting up the number of tracts that each of us dishes out, we are in trouble. We are in trouble any time we start to set up a standard for all others rather than to receive from God that which he wants to give us, in all fairness, individually.

Each of us is called individually to do his own thing well. The rich to be rich, the poor to be poor, the married to be married, the unmarried to be unmarried, and we are not to feel sorry for ourselves.

Even in our suffering, even in our imperfections, we must look first to God rather than to our neighbor. For if we look to our neighbor, then we may see the suffering as God's insufficient love rather than as a result of the Fall and the general brokenness of all reality.

If I look at myself, I see that I have to wear glasses and I can't swim the way I used to be able to swim. And I can't come off the diving board any more because it is very difficult with glasses. If I set this up as an absolute, then I become jealous of all of those who do not have to wear glasses, and that is wrong. I could sit up in my room all day long and feel sorry for myself. If Abigail had felt sorry for herself and had wanted to protect her position, things would not have turned out the way God wanted them to turn out, which was to her advantage.

When we understand how much God gives us and when we understand that our call is to be faithful to that which he has called us into, then we are free to start looking at each other. Then we can begin to practice the care of each other and even to rejoice with others when they have more than we do. We get more of a feel for the totality of man and for the fallenness of history and for all the suffering that is in the world. Then we will not be looking at ourselves and feeling dreadfully sorry. Then we will see how much God gives us, how really good God is to us individually. We will see that other people are depressed and other people are tired and other people have problems, and we can come together to God and share, not by comparing ourselves with others but by rejoicing in the things God has given to each of us. We can begin to rejoice with thanksgiving because life as God granted it to us is indeed good. And of course the Christian has a unique hope. He looks forward to the ultimate removal of all trouble, all imperfection, all tears and all death.

All this is so well expressed in Psalm 73 that I would like to include this entire psalm here and encourage you to read it and reread it, even to pray your way through it to help to reorient your life so that God is truly at the center.

Truly God is good to the upright,
to those who are pure in heart.
But as for me, my feet had almost stumbled,
my steps had well nigh slipped.
For I was envious of the arrogant,
when I saw the prosperity of the wicked.

For they have no pangs;
their bodies are sound and sleek.
They are not in trouble as other men are;
they are not stricken like other men.
Therefore pride is their necklace;
violence covers them as a garment.
Their eyes swell out with fatness,
their hearts overflow with follies.
They scoff and speak with malice;
loftily they threaten oppression.
They set their mouths against the heavens,
and their tongue struts through the earth.

Therefore the people turn and praise them;
and find no fault in them.
And they say, "How can God know?
Is there knowledge in the Most High?"
Behold, these are the wicked;
always at ease, they increase in riches.
All in vain have I kept my heart clean
and washed my hands in innocence.
For all the day long I have been stricken,
and chastened every morning.

If I had said, "I will speak thus,"
I would have been untrue to the generation of thy
children.
But when I thought how to understand this,

it seemed to me a wearisome task,
until I went into the sanctuary of God;
then I perceived their end.

Truly thou dost set them in slippery places;
thou dost make them fall to ruin.
How they are destroyed in a moment,
swept away utterly by terrors!
They are like a dream when one awakes,
on awaking you despise their phantoms.

When my soul was embittered,
when I was pricked in heart,
I was stupid and ignorant,
I was like a beast toward thee.
Nevertheless I am continually with thee;
thou dost hold my right hand.
Thou dost guide me with thy counsel,
and afterward thou wilt receive me to glory.
Whom have I in heaven but thee?
And there is nothing upon earth that I desire
besides thee.
My flesh and my heart may fail,
but God is the strength of my heart and my portion
for ever.

For lo, those who are far from thee shall perish;
thou dost put an end to those who are false to thee.
But for me it is good to be near God;
I have made the Lord GOD my refuge,
that I may tell of all thy works.

Let us enlarge our vision by making God the center of
all reality. Looking to God does not remove the painful-
ness of pain, but it gives us a perspective outside of ourselves in which to understand that pain. Looking to God
reveals the limits of selfishness. Looking to God helps us

understand that we live in a fallen world, it helps see why in losing our life we find it. In taking up our cross we recognize our brokenness and we receive the answers that come from Christ and his work in history. Looking to God enables us to live in the hope of the redemption and the restoration and the perfection of not only ourselves but of all that is God's. Only when we look at God can we see ourselves as we really are.

Pro-Existence and the Return of the King

"It is only when I demonstrate my willingness to obey civil authorities that my disobedience on the basis of God's commands can possibly be interpreted as other than selfishness, disinterest or cowardice. Obedience forms the backdrop against which disobedience can be meaningful and can display a greater sense of goodness, justice and morality than obedience itself. Only by obedience do I earn the right to disobey."

5

Following Christ means to take up our cross daily, to lose our life, to abandon the egocentric existence in which we set ourselves up as arbiters of truth and lords of our own life. Moses, David, Solomon, Jonah and Elijah illustrate what happens not when we are introspective but when we turn and follow God. The same principle applies to the relationship of man and the state.

Many young people today find it easy to leave their country whenever the going gets rough. With air fares across the Atlantic so reasonable, it is easy to escape and to be treated in a European country as a guest. But isn't this another area in which we are asserting ourselves as lords of our own lives, escaping from a tight spot rather than working in it and losing ourselves in the midst of it?

People in totalitarian countries have no such option. The government restricts travel and people are forced to make do where they are. We, too, in the area of man-to-man relationships and man-to-state relationships, must be willing to lose our lives in order to gain them, not just in theological terms but in practice.

The World around Us

The problem of how a Christian is to live in society has become especially important in recent years. There are several reasons for this. First, the communications media make the faults of men better known. When we lived in little villages, we knew what went wrong in the village but not what went wrong in the larger world. We could be idealistic about the "outside." We could even dream of escaping from our village and thus from our problems.

Now all the horror of man is brought immediately into our living rooms, and we know much more about how so many people are mixed up, how so many people are oppressed, how so many people have the same problems we do in our own "village." Government actions around the world are seen together and all at once. We feel under tremendous pressure: So many evil things, such a corrupted world!

Second, as science has developed, so has man's potential to destroy. New techniques become immediately available, and, in the absence of a sufficient general moral framework that would control their use, their availability exerts a psychological pressure on a technological society to use them regardless of the result. Science is a good thing in itself. By it we discover how the universe is made and are supplied with information which we can use for constructive purposes. But science has brought with it potential for more and more destructive action. Science is getting away from us, making us more inhuman.

Third, we are finding not only the growing sophistication of man but also his growing cruelty toward his fellow man. All of the emphasis that increased education will diminish the evil that exists is absolute rubbish in the face of recent history, for we have come to see that the more man knows the more cruel he becomes. George Steiner dares to publish what was recognized in secret, that "in our own day the high places of literacy, of philosophy, of artistic expression, became the setting for Belsen [the concentration camp]. . . . The house of classic humanism, the dream of reason which animated Western society, have largely broken down."[1] Goya entitled one of his etchings with words born out of a similar recognition: "The Dream of Reason Produces Monsters."

Fourth, we have developed a perverted sense of history. Instant enjoyment is the goal. When I do not instantly receive what I want, then indeed I opt out or throw things. I revolt. That work takes time, that healing is rarely immediate or perfect, that growth is gradual, that reform may be a long process: These ideas are far removed from the modern mentality.

Because the objective view of reality and the objective framework for morals are gone, these four tendencies—and I could mention more—lead to violence, a violence that is often coupled with sheer idealism. This idealism takes two forms: (1) establishment idealism in which nothing wrong is seen in the established order or (2) revolutionary idealism in which solutions are sought outside reality altogether, as we shall see below. In both forms, the perverted sense of history prevails and there is a tendency for us to use violence to further our selfish desires. What matters is that we have what we want—and have it now.

Both the idealism of the established order that says everything is all right when it is not and the idealism of those who with violence try to gain perfection at this moment are really an expression of the same basic problem—the selfishness of man.

The reality that exists is not just what I experience. As long as I set myself up as God, the only reality that I know is my immediate perception, and it is always limited and often wrong. I need something larger, something objective. It is here that the Bible is valuable, for it gives answers that come from God before whom all reality is fully known and understood.

A Biblical Perspective

The Bible presents God's prescription for living in today's world because it gives God's law for fallen man. When God's creation was still beautiful, when God in his perfect character looked upon it and said, "Behold, it is very good," there was no Bible. The Bible came only after the Fall. So God's law in the Bible takes into consideration the brokenness of the world and tells us who to be and what to do. When we listen to the Creator speaking into his fallen creation, we can know that it is not just our present experience of imperfection that is speaking to us but that he who knows the background of all reality fully understands us and therefore is not giving us naive, idealistic advice.

Moreover, the Bible warns us that we will always be obliged to live in a less than perfect situation. The standard set forth is always perfection, and indeed Christ will eventually bring about that perfection. Something of this has already been achieved in the relationship of man to God through the work of Christ on the cross for those individuals who accept it personally. But the work of perfection will only be completed at Christ's second coming. Until then there will be tears, there will be death, there will be imperfection.

The idea that we can by our own effort bring about a perfect society or a perfect man is blindly naive. True, we are to work toward perfection, for God's standard is never less than that. But we must know that the Bible does not promise this perfection until Christ returns as King of Kings and Lord of Lords.

Order Is Better than Chaos

Living in the reality bounded by this perspective means

several things. It means, first, that order is better than chaos. As Calvin said, "However corrupt the government be, God never suffers it to be so much so as not to be better than anarchy."[2] Tyranny harasses many, but anarchy overwhelms the whole of society including the anarchists.

It is against the background of this principle that the Bible emphasizes over and over that the individual Christian must be subject to the authorities. The Bible is not idealistic about authorities. It does not say that when you are subject to the authorities you will have a perfect situation or that the authorities themselves are perfect. Absolutely no one is perfect. Still, until Christ returns, we must be in subjection to the authorities.

This attitude begins early in Scripture. In the passage following the Ten Commandments in Exodus, we read: "You shall not revile God, nor curse a ruler of your people" (Ex. 22:28). This admonition was carried out in practice by Paul when he was dragged before the Sanhedrin, supposedly because he desecrated the Jewish temple by bringing Gentiles into it.

And Paul, looking intently at the council, said, "Brethren, I have lived before God in all good conscience up to this day." And the high priest Ananias commanded those who stood by him to strike him on the mouth. Then Paul said to him, "God shall strike you, you whitewashed wall! Are you sitting to judge me according to the law, and yet contrary to the law you order me to be struck?" Those who stood by said, "Would you revile God's high priest?" And Paul said, "I did not know, brethren, that he was the high priest; for it is written, 'You shall not speak evil of a ruler of your people.'" (Acts 23:1-5)

It is hard to respect such authorities. But the Bible teaches us to be a little less selfish, to be subject to the rulers that are there, not because the rulers give a perfect order but because any order is better than chaos.

109

Other verses give us the same instruction. "Even in your thought, do not curse the king, nor in your bedchamber curse the rich; for a bird of the air will carry your voice, or some winged creature tell the matter" (Eccles. 10:20). And "Keep the king's command, and because of your sacred oath be not dismayed; go from his presence, do not delay when the matter is unpleasant, for he does whatever he pleases. For the word of the king is supreme, and who may say to him, 'What are you doing?' He who obeys a command will meet no harm, and the mind of a wise man will know the time and way" (Eccles. 8:2-5). In the New Testament we find Paul writing to Titus, "Remind them [the church in Crete] to be submissive to rulers and authorities, to be obedient, to be ready for any honest work. . . ." (Tit. 3:1).

There are two passages, however, which are most often quoted in this connection. The first is in 1 Peter.

Be subject for the Lord's sake to every human institution, whether it be to the emperor as supreme, or to governors as sent by him to punish those who do wrong and to praise those who do right. For it is God's will that by doing right you should put to silence the ignorance of foolish men. Live as free men, yet without using your freedom as a pretext for evil; but live as servants of God. Honour all men. Love the brotherhood. Fear God. Honour the emporer.

Servants, be submissive to your masters with all respect, not only to the kind and gentle but also to the overbearing. For one is approved if, mindful of God, he endures pain while suffering unjustly. (1 Pet. 2:13-19)

The second passage is in Paul's letter to the Romans.

Let every person be subject to the governing authorities. For there is no authority except from God, and those that exist have been instituted by God. Therefore he who resists the authorities resists what God has appointed, and those who resist will incur judgment. For rulers are not a terror to good conduct, but to bad. Would you have no fear of him who is in authority? Then do what is good, and you will receive his approval, for he is God's servant for your good. But if you do wrong, be afraid, for he does not bear the sword in vain; he is the servant of God to execute his wrath on the wrongdoer. Therefore one must be subject, not only to avoid God's wrath but also for the sake of conscience. For the same reason you also pay taxes, for the authorities are ministers of God, attending to this very thing. Pay all of them their dues, taxes to whom taxes are due, revenue to whom revenue is due, respect to whom respect is due, honour to whom honour is due.

Owe no one anything, except to love one another; for he who loves his neighbour has fulfilled the law. The commandments, "You shall not commit adultery, You shall not kill, You shall not steal, You shall not covet," and any other commandment, are summed up in this sentence, "You shall love your neighbour as yourself." Love does no wrong to a neighbour; therefore love is the fulfilling of the law. (Rom. 13:1-10)

Why are we to submit to the authorities? Why are both Peter and Paul so adamant? Peter writes that we are to submit to the authorities "for the Lord's sake" (1 Pet. 2:13), and Paul says that we are to do it not only to avoid God's wrath but also "for the sake of conscience" (Rom. 13:5). The reality that exists is a reality in which God not man is at the center. Therefore the command to obey the authorities must be seen not only in the context of the immediate need to make a decision to obey or not to obey but in the total reality where God is seen as Lord of all history and where his will may include obedience to authorities who are not themselves in subjection to him. Both of these passages, therefore, boil down to this: Out of a conscientious regard for God, not for men, we are to be sub-

111

ject to the authorities.

Furthermore, the advice reflects the profound understanding that bad government is better than no government. Young people often shrug their shoulders and say, "Well, our government is certainly worse than a 'bad' government." Each says it for his own country. But they are wrong.

I once talked to a pastor in Holland whose father had been killed in the Buchenwald concentration camp. Most people know something of the situations in the Nazi concentration camps, and no one would minimize their inhumanity. But this pastor said that there was a greater humanness among the inmates of Buchenwald while they waited for the gas chamber than during the period after the Nazis had fled from the onmarching Allied troops and before the Allies opened up the camp. For a day and a half there was pure anarchy; some inmates had even turned to cannibalism. Let us not be naive. In a fallen universe, it is better to have a bad government than no government at all.

No king was ever approved of by all his subjects. Often we would like to replace him. We all have aspirations and longings to go beyond the present situation and we try to fulfill these aspirations. But the way to do so is not to be driven by false idealism and violence.

The writer of Ecclesiastes reflected on "life under the sun," the dilemma of the world without God, this way: "Better is a poor and wise youth than an old and foolish king, who will no longer take advice, even though he had gone from prison to the throne or in his own kingdom had been born poor. I saw all the living who move about under the sun, as well as that youth, who was to stand in his place; there was no end of all the people; he was over all of them. Yet those who come later will not rejoice in him. Surely this also is vanity and a striving after wind" (Eccles. 4:13-16). To imagine that a king is ever going to be perfect is indeed vanity and striving after wind. One king may be no better than another.

Surely, one may say at this point, "If order is better than chaos and bad government is better than no government, there is nothing that a Christian can do." Nothing could be further from the truth. We do not need to be content with the status quo or to call that which is bad good. God's standard is perfection.

Idealistic Answers

The question is, Is our desire for change idealistic and man-centered? Or is it focused on God as the center of reality and the standard of perfection? The two starting points are totally different, and so are the results. As long as man idealistically begins only with himself and his own private world view, whether in politics or in religion, he will not arrive at a perfect solution. The context is not big enough; the solutions can only be temporary.

Just before he was to die, Peter warned the church about man-centered solutions:

> But false prophets also arose among the people, just as there will be false teachers among you, who will secretly bring in destructive heresies, even denying the Master who bought them, bringing upon themselves swift destruction. And many will follow their licentiousness, and because of them the way of truth will be reviled. And in their greed they will exploit you with false words; from of old their condemnation has not been idle, and their destruction has not been asleep. (2 Pet. 2:1-3)

Verse 10 mentions "especially those who indulge in the lust of defiling passion and despise authority," and verse 12 mentions men "like irrational animals, creatures of instinct, born to be caught and killed, reviling in matters of which they are ignorant, [that] will be destroyed in the same destruction. . . ." Jude likewise speaks of men who

113

"in their dreamings defile the flesh, reject authority, and revile the glorious ones," reviling "whatever they do not understand" (Jude 8, 10).

Peter and Jude are both speaking of exactly the same people, men who begin with themselves and their own imaginations. Jude says that they are the ones who "dream." There is a double meaning here. There are dreams we dream in darkness as we sleep and dreams we dream in spiritual darkness as a result of our own mind's imagination. In both cases the answers are subjective imaginations.

But a dream is a dream. It will never stand up to the totality of the real world in which we have to live.

Take the world that is entered through drugs. Why couldn't one go into the desert, cut himself off from everyone and have a perfect drug trip? For one thing, someone would have to drop water to you. You always take your mannishness with you. You would have to wipe out your own footsteps, because you are a man even when you go into the most empty desert. We have to live in the real world, not just in the world we conjure up.

Second, we tend to see injustice not in the total flow of history, but only in terms of the present. On a broad scale history can show us this. The French Revolution, for example, began as a rebellion against the atrocity and tyranny of the French kings. The revolutionaries saw the injustice, they acted to remove it, but they did not anticipate the consequences because their perspective was too narrow. The fact is that more people died in the Revolution than in the preceding century.

On a personal level, this expresses itself in the following "reasoning": I feel sorrow because I am hurt or have pain at this individual moment, but I do not see that the universe as a whole is abnormal. I revolt, and I do not take into consideration what I produce by my revolt. A loss of historical perspective, that after the Fall all life is imperfect, makes most of my solutions unrealistic. I either have forgotten that we cannot have an ideal answer in a corrupted, fallen world or I have never read history. How can we trust our own idealism or any man's answer once we understand something of man's past?

Third, idealism tends to lead to the place where men are willing to fight injustice with injustice. When Lenin was in Lausanne in 1917, he spoke of his desire to bring about what Marx called the classless society: "When the Revolution comes, we must have no companions. We must destroy without pity." In many ways Lenin's ideal was good. But if man alone chooses his own ideals and his own ways of achieving them, his selfishness will actually poison his own ideals. He may well end up in the horrible dilemma of having to fight injustice with injustice. If one pursues his ideal at all cost, he will tend to invest everything that leads to the fulfillment of that ideal with moral goodness, even at the price of humanness or life itself.

The Christian Stance
How is a Christian to respond, then, to the world's glaring imperfection? Three things are involved.

One of the things we are to do is to pray for our country, for our leaders, for men in high places, so that we may lead a tranquil life. Paul writes, "First of all, then, I urge that supplications, prayers, intercessions, and thanksgivings be made for all men, for kings and all who are in high positions, that we may lead a quiet and peaceable life, godly and respectful in every way. This is good, and it is acceptable in the sight of God our Saviour, who desires all men to be saved and to come to the knowledge of the truth" (1 Tim. 2:1-4). We ought not to look for an ideal life, not until Christ comes back, but we can look forward to a certain degree of tranquility so that our existence as Christians is not impeded by either disorder or tyranny.

115

Second, we are to take a realistic view of history. If I understand that I must be obedient to the state because all reality is broken and any government is better than no government, I can afford to be a bit more confident and react from a wider angle. I no longer have to follow my dreams (which have no connection to reality) and be crushed when they are not fulfilled. Neither do I have to resign myself to the present as the best of all possible solutions.

All reality is broken, my problems are not the only problems, my government is not the only corrupt government. I can look at birth and enjoy it. I can look at death and weep. I can face both as real. I can face death as abnormal. I do not have to take the Buddha's way out, saying that a baby crying at birth and the corpse of a dead man are opposites only in my mind. I can distinguish between beauty and ugliness. These opposites are real, and I can admit them.

I can even be encouraged that I am not alone in sorrow but that God is also in sorrow over the fallenness of his creation. More than that, I can face all of history because I do not have to be idealistic about man and his solutions.

All human communities are fallen. So I do not have to be blind in order to hold on to an idealistic view of my community or my church or my friends. And yet a true Christian community can witness to the fact that while men are not perfect God is involved and will continue to be involved in substantial healing. By expressing love and compassion in concrete ways—feeding the hungry, accepting the lonely, helping the helpless—the Christian community can show that the real answers come from God, not man. That is, we are to show forth God's victory in the circumference of our lives.

Third, we are to show forth God's victory even in our death. Hebrews 11 lists and describes briefly many heroes of the faith who showed God's victory and healing in their lives. Their stories in the Old Testament make exciting reading. But in the latter part of Hebrews 11 we find people who showed forth God's victory and healing only through their death:

Some were tortured, refusing to accept release, that they might rise again to a better life. Others suffered mocking and scourging, and even chains and imprisonment. They were stoned, they were sawn in two, they were killed with the sword; they went about in skins of sheep and goats, destitute, afflicted, ill-treated —of whom the world was not worthy—wandering over deserts and mountains, and in dens and caves of the earth. (Heb. 11:35-38)

What then does it mean to show forth God's victory and healing in my life and my death? It means basically giving up selfishness. It means being content with God, being proud of God and proud of the fact that God wants to use us to show that he is there. It means we must be willing to live as Christians in a less than perfect society even when it requires our death, looking forward to the perfection that will come when Christ returns. This way we will be able to work in the total flow of history and not be discouraged when there are no immediate results. We can work for twenty years to achieve something of beauty. And there is value in this because it stands as a symbol of God's victory which will be complete when Christ returns.

Pro-Existence

Thus, Christians should become an undercurrent, permeating all of society and speaking and living for God. In one East European country, the term *pro-existence* was coined to label the task of Christians in a totally materialistic society. In a political framework which brands them as the weakest of men, they are endeavoring to exhibit real humanness by their affirmation of honesty, love,

117

family pride and strength of character. As Christians, they are for existence. They are called as God's children to live in the corrupted, broken world and to show forth the character of God by placing him in the center of their lives. They are attempting to permeate society with its false values and false ideals and to become a living an-swer to the questions society has.

Pro-existence indicates that they are for all areas of life. They seek to establish a Christian affirmation to life in a materialistic society against the misrepresentation that religion is the opiate of the people or harmful to the state. In a living way they seek to fight social injustice and the pervading nihilism and thus to disprove the state's accusation and to demonstrate in a tangible fashion that all barriers are gone—the barrier of both class and social distinctions. They seek to demonstrate that charity and real peace can exist and to visibly show an alternative to the attitudes of the surrounding materialistic society. As Christians they are for man not against him.

What does pro-existence then mean in a non-commu-nist society, a situation in which there is yet a legacy of human dignity on Christian terms? Certainly it means that one should recognize injustice where it exists, though it also means not expecting to be able to produce the millenium by our efforts and on our own time sched-ule. It means that our master for our thinking and our action must be our master in heaven. He alone can give us the sufficient perspective for our action on earth.

Pro-existence means that I will always fight for greater freedoms in an age of increasing structuralization of society. I will live my family life as a visible representation of true community, strive to help my church be a model community on a larger scale, act as a citizen—to vote, to serve on local governing boards, perhaps even to enter the political arena itself. In short, it means being a re-sponsible member of society. This will require a willingness to limit my selfishness for the benefit of a more human situation for myself and others.

To that extent pro-existence means that I should normally choose obedience to the authorities, recognizing, of course, that my responsibility includes evaluating the existing authority and striving to keep or bring about a proper basis and character for that authority. Pro-existence may indeed involve conflict with the existing authorities. But it does not deny the necessity for authority itself.

There is, however, an important limitation to a Christian's obedience to the authorities. A Christian can never obey the earthly authorities when it means disobeying a clear commandment of God. This was the situation faced by Peter in Acts 4 when he and the other apostles were commanded not to tell the truth of what they had seen and experienced. Peter's response was categorical: "Whether it is right in the sight of God to listen to you rather than to God, you must judge; for we cannot but speak of what we have seen and heard" (Acts 4:19-20).

The same applies when we rebel against the evil in society. We are to be for man because he is made in the image of God. So we must be careful not to fight injustice by injustice or death by death. We cannot resist the attack on man for the sake of some supposed "good," in the manner, say, of the Eastern religions which deny the mannishness of man, or in the manner of modern revolutionaries who in their violence destroy man, or in the name of the technocracy that reduces man to a machine. We must not fight man in the name of Man.

In the Third Reich it was legal to kill the enemies of the state. The Jews were considered to be the biggest enemies, and it was perfectly legal to exterminate them, and so this was done in a very orderly fashion. Christians are not against man made in the image of God, but against all gods that man has made in his own image, including the

119

god of goodness or justice or law or order. When such gods rule a state, Christians must unmask the evil and fight for man. Disobedience may then be the only possible Christian response. But it is only when I demonstrate my willingness to obey that my disobedience on the basis of God's commands can possibly be interpreted as other than selfishness, disinterest or cowardice. Obedience forms the backdrop against which disobedience can be meaningful and can display a greater sense of goodness, justice and morality than obedience itself. Only by obedience do I earn the right to disobey.

This is the very opposite of what we often find today in the application of "civil disobedience." The movement is characterized by the absence of any notion of authority or limitation on selfishness. That is, structure as a category is denied; form is seen as a violation of freedom rather than as the boundary within which a true freedom which does not violate the rights of others can be established.

The Return of the King
In Psalm 2, the rulers of the earth take counsel together against "the LORD and his anointed" and say, "Let us burst their bonds asunder, and cast their cords from us" (v. 3). That is, the nations want to free themselves from the law of God and from his being the center of their existence. Yet the psalmist says,

He who sits in the heavens laughs;
   the LORD has them in derision.
Then he will speak to them in his wrath,
   and terrify them in his fury, saying,
"I have set my king
   on Zion, my holy hill."
I will tell of the decree of the LORD:
He said to me, "You are my son,
   today I have begotten you." (Ps. 2:4-7)

When the nations conspire, God is not undone. But he sends his solution to men's problems in his own way. The real solution is the coming of the Messiah.

In Acts 4 we find the same mentality expressed by the early church. When Peter and John were ordered by the Sanhedrin not to speak of God any more, the disciples got together and praised God in their prayer, saying,

> Sovereign Lord, who didst make the heaven and the earth and the sea and everything in them, who by the mouth of our father David, thy servant, didst say by the Holy Spirit,
>
> "Why did the Gentiles rage,
> and the peoples imagine vain things?
> The kings of the earth set themselves in array,
> and the rulers were gathered together,
> against the Lord and against his Anointed"—
>
> for truly in this city there were gathered together against thy holy servant Jesus, whom thou didst anoint, both Herod and Pontius Pilate, with the Gentiles and the peoples of Israel, to do whatever thy hand and thy plan had predestined to take place. (Acts 4:24-28)

The Christians lived in a situation in which men had set themselves against God, but they recognized that God was the destroyer of these evil plans. In pro-existence we are to permeate all society and be an undercurrent of real Christian existence both as individuals and in communities. Pro-existence is, in short, the present expression of the anticipation of the return of the king.

We are to speak for God against evil, but not selfishly. We are to show the basis upon which our statements are made. We are to show in a living way that God is God, to speak out against evil, and in the reality of our Christian life together show how injustice can be healed, the hungry fed and wrongs righted. The revolution must be God's revolution, and it must be done in God's way.

121

This includes the knowledge that, when the people of God cry unto him, he will hear their cry. It's instructive to take a concordance and go through the Bible, noting all the places where it says that the people of God cried unto the Lord. In Judges, the people of Israel had sinned and God had brought down hard judgment on them. So they cried to the Lord for twenty years, and God finally raised up a judge and liberated them.

The message is the same throughout the Scripture, in Exodus, in Judges, in Psalms, in the whole Old Testament and the New. Cry unto the Lord, and the Lord will hear you. Let selflessness mean only the desire to live in God's reality. Let it mean that we cry to God to see his salvation. But the manifestation of things we cry for often takes years to come, not because God does not hear our cry but because history is real and because God does not undo injustice by injustice.

So we are to trust God and work toward the coming of Christ as King of Kings at the head of his army, the head of the church. We are to work against the foundations of modern society, its commercialism, its materialism, and to show our care for man the way Christ did who came to die for man to make him more man, not less.

We are to lose our self-centeredness, perhaps even our physical life, but we shall have gained it here and more in the world to come. We will not be able to achieve perfection. But in practice let our whole life, in the situations in which we find ourselves, "show forth Christ's death until he come," not calling evil good, not being idealistic by thinking the evil is so small it is not worth fighting against or thinking we can achieve perfection ourselves. God has promised his perfection when the King returns. That provides the dynamic for our lives and validates our hope.

Notes

chapter 1
1/ Jacques Ellul, "Work and Calling," *Katallagete* (Fall-Winter 1972), p. 13.
2/ Ibid., pp. 13-14.
3/ Ibid., p. 14.
4/ Ibid., p. 9.
5/ Ibid., p. 10.
6/ Ibid.
7/ Ibid., p. 14.
8/ Ibid.
9/ "Is the Work Ethic Going Out of Style?" *Time* magazine (October 30, 1972), pp. 96-97.

chapter 3
1/ Eric Heller, *Thomas Mann: The Ironic German* (New York: Little, Brown, 1958), p. 84.
2/ *The Westminster Larger Catechism, 1648* (London: Blackwood and Sons, 1963), questions 6 and 7; and Francis A. Schaeffer, *Escape from Reason* (Downers Grove, Ill.: InterVarsity Press, 1968), p. 21.

125

3/ Sir Peter Medawar, "The Effecting of All Things Possible," *The Listener* (October 2, 1969), p. 438.

4/ See, for example, Hans Koningsberger, *The World of Vermeer 1632-1675* (New York: Time-Life, 1967).

5/ Julien Benda, *Treason of the Intellectuals,* trans. Richard Aldington (New York: Norton Press, 1969).

6/ Heller, p. 83.

7/ Ibid., p. 84.

8/ Ibid., p. 83.

9/ Medawar, p. 438.

10 "Discourse on Method, Part IV," in *The Philosophical Works of Descartes* (New York: Dover Publications, 1955), II, 101.

11/ Ibid.

12/ Ibid., "Meditation I," p. 145.

13/ Ibid.

14/ Ibid., pp. 145-46.

15/ Hans Sedlmayr, *Verlust der Mitte (The Loss of Center)* (West Berlin:) Ullstein Verlag, 1966), p. 135. "Im Pantheismus und Deismus des 18. Jahrhunderts wird eine Kluft zwischen Gott und dem Menschen aufgerissen. Zunächst scheint die Idee Gottes viel reiner und erhabener als die des persönlichen Gottes. Man treibt aus der Idee von Gott das scheinbar Anthropomorphe ... aus. ... Aber dieser Gott der Philosophen löst sich damit in die Natur auf und verschwindet. Und zugleich nimmt man dem Menschen das Theomorphe, das Gottförmige, und schraubt ihn damit—obwohl man die Reinheit des Menschentums herzustellen meint—zurück auf die Rolle von Automat und Dämon." (In the pantheism and deism of the 18th century a chasm is torn open between God and man. At first, the idea of God appears much purer and loftier than the idea of the personal God. One removes from the idea of God the apparently anthropomorphic. ... But this God of the philosophers thus dissolves in nature and disappears. And at the same time one removes from man the theomorphic, the god-likeness, and reduces him to the role of the automatic or demonic, though believing to produce the purity of mannishness.)

16/ Juan C. Mesas, "Historiography in the Light of Golgotha," *Salt* (Covenant Theological Seminary, St. Louis), 2 (Summer 1972), p. 2.

17/ Ibid.

18/ George Steiner, *Language and Silence: Essays on Language, Literature, and the Inhuman* (New York: Atheneum, 1967), p. x.

19/ Ibid., p. 21.

20/ Hermann Hesse, *Journey to the East* (New York: Noonday Press, 1970), p. 52, for example.

chapter 5

1/ Steiner, p. ix.

2/ Quoted by Jamieson, Fausset and Brown, *Commentary on the Bible* (London: Oliphants, Ltd., 1959) in reference to 1 Pet. 2:14.